MONEY
MALOCCLUSION

MONEY
MALOCCLUSION

Tools *and* **Strategies**
for **Dentists** *to* **Align**
Practice *and* **Personal Goals**

JAKE JACKLICH CFP®

Published by Advantage, Charleston, South Carolina.
Member of Advantage Media Group.

ADVANTAGE is a registered trademark and the Advantage colophon is a trademark of Advantage Media Group, Inc.

Printed in the United States of America.

ISBN: 978-1-59932-530-9
LCCN: 2015944937

This publication is designed to provide accurate and authoritative information in regard to the subject matter covered. It is sold with the understanding that the publisher is not engaged in rendering legal, accounting, or other professional services. If legal advice or other expert assistance is required, the services of a competent professional person should be sought.

Advantage Media Group is proud to be a part of the Tree Neutral® program. Tree Neutral offsets the number of trees consumed in the production and printing of this book by taking proactive steps such as planting trees in direct proportion to the number of trees used to print books. To learn more about Tree Neutral, please visit **www.treeneutral.com**. To learn more about Advantage's commitment to being a responsible steward of the environment, please visit **www.advantagefamily.com/green**

Advantage Media Group is a publisher of business, self-improvement, and professional development books and online learning. We help entrepreneurs, business leaders, and professionals share their Stories, Passion, and Knowledge to help others Learn & Grow. Do you have a manuscript or book idea that you would like us to consider for publishing? Please visit **advantagefamily.com** or call **1.866.775.1696.**

TABLE OF CONTENTS

*This book is dedicated to my clients and those
I serve in the dental profession.*

ACKNOWLEDGMENTS

I gratefully acknowledge the collective wisdom of those who have attended and shared their insight at my monthly Dental Business Network lunches over the last decade. I truly appreciate your diverse wisdom and technical knowledge.

Special thanks to Attorney Edwin Greene who helped tremendously with the chapter on estate planning and asset protection strategies.

Certified Public Accounts Nicole Wood-Sabo and Robert Carmines have been invaluable with all things tax related.

Banker Stephen Trutter was a terrific resource for all things related to a dentist's business debt and its pitfalls.

Special thanks to Linda Cannon, the great connector who literally knows everyone who is relevant in the dental industry today.

I also want to acknowledge the work of the country's dental practice management consultants. This work has resulted in much more than efficiency and prosperity—they bring out the best of doctors and team members to raise the standard of care for all patients.

I want to thank Scott J. Manning MBA, Darren Kaberna, and Jonathan Van Horn CPA for their work to improve cash flow and business profit from within the dental practice.

Lastly, I want to thank Linda Miles, whose enthusiasm for thinking big and for dental success inspired me for nearly a decade.

TIME FOR A CHECKUP

You have worked hard for years to build a thriving dental practice. One day, a new patient comes in, complaining of a toothache. Do you get out the forceps and start pulling out what might be the offending tooth? Or do you first do an overall assessment of the patient's oral health?

It's hard to imagine that any dentist would reach for the forceps without examining the whole mouth, the gum line, and the tissues beneath. It's important to see how it all fits together. This calls for X-rays and probing. The patient needs to hear all relevant options and decide on the best treatment plan.

And yet, when it comes to their own financial health, dentists all over the country just start yanking without a process to examine the underlying issues. Some try to handle their own financial affairs—taking out loans, investing, and buying insurance—as if they were engaging in do-it-yourself dentistry.

If that describes you, be careful. You could end up in a lot more financial pain than you expect. By nature, you are probably pragmatic, like most dentists. You look for solutions, evaluate options, and generally make smart choices. You have two financial lives, one business and one personal. You need to apply that type of decision process to your business and personal financial life, too. Snap decisions on one side of your life could create big problems or reduce options on the other side.

You need regular assessments of where you are and what you want to achieve so that you can devise a congruent strategy for your business and personal goals. Each decision impacts your current situation and your future. Those decisions interrelate. It's much more complicated than dealing with financial issues independently, as in: "I'm going to buy a big house," or "I'm going to get a business loan," or "I'm going to set up a 401(k) plan."

This book is meant to help the American General Dentist better frame and prioritize the financial issues associated with personal and professional goal pursuit. It emphasizes the importance of financial congruency between the dental practice and the doctor's personal finances. There's a lot of room to do a better job and get a potentially better outcome if you just step back and look at the bigger picture rather than going for the quick fix.

A UNIQUE SPECIALTY

I am one of the few CERTIFIED FINANCIAL PLANNER™ Professionals who specialize in working with dentists. I have written articles that focus on the dental profession, and other financial planners have sought me out for advice on cases for their clients who are dentists. My hope is that this book will serve you, the dentist, and those who offer dentists advice about business and personal finances.

Dentists face unique issues and opportunities. You need a financial advisor who is sensitive to the specific hazards that tend to trip up a lot of dentists and prevent them from achieving the success that they sought. As you know, it's possible to have poor oral health while having individually healthy teeth. In my experience, most dentists are either getting uncoordinated service from their advisors or are trying to do the job themselves and failing to get the perspective they need. They need to see both opportunities and pitfalls—and that's difficult for a do-it-yourselfer.

You may be among the best of dentists, but I am sure that you don't work on your own teeth. You find a trusted colleague for that sort of care. You should feel the same way about your financial affairs. You have a better shot of doing a successful root canal in your own mouth than you do of achieving your most important financial goals on your own. You are aware of your limitations in being your own dentist. Are you aware of your limitations in being your own financial advisor?

What dentists need today is somebody who will keep them on track when things are going well and will talk them off the ledge when they are about to make a bad choice. If you are acting as your own financial advisor, nobody will do that for you. You need a guide who cares about you and your family. Otherwise, in your next rough spot, you might do something unwise or do nothing when action is critical.

You certainly are smart enough to handle money, but, like many dentists, you may lack the perspective to analyze the choices and make the right call without bias or emotion. Working with someone who has experience and knows you well is often the difference between success and failure.

From a big-picture perspective, it's important to look at proper use of your financial resources, time, and money from the correct perspective. It's vital that you emphasize the correct financial planning strategy for your situation. Your situation changes over time, but there are a couple of times when you really need to change your strategic mindset and how you utilize your resources. The first change comes when you initially become a dental practice owner. The second strategic shift comes when you begin the multiyear process of transitioning your business. The third shift comes when you stop practicing dentistry and learn to live comfortably off the income derived from those assets that you have accumulated throughout the arc of your career.

OPPORTUNITIES AND OBSTACLES

As a dentist, you may have a lot of the same concerns as other small-business owners—your family, patients, and staff. You want to grow your practice. And you are troubled about whether you are doing enough and minimizing your risks. You need an adviser who will cover those bases first and then focus on the traditional topics of financial planning.

As recently as 2012 about 84.8% of dentists surveyed by the ADA reported being practice owners.[1] The typical dentist makes between $100,000 and $250,000 a year, but there's a big difference between having a lot of money coming in and being okay financially.

Dentists, as you may know all too well, have a tendency to pay themselves last, after the staff, the office rent or mortgage and electric bills, the equipment loans, the suppliers, and the computer guy. Any money left after paying these necessities goes to covering personal mortgages, student loan debt, or, perhaps, a much-needed vacation.

Dentists make good money, but with all of these expenses, saving enough to retire is a challenge. Dentistry is capital intensive. It takes a lot of money to operate a practice, and you may find yourself with a large business loan. The changing tax environment doesn't help.

You have to find the money to save, invest, and cover risks with various insurances—life, disability, and business. That's critical in the first half of a dental career. Once you have accumulated a decent nest egg and have built a thriving practice, you need to position yourself and your business to get out of dentistry and move onward to the next part of your life. But how do you transfer your business, take care of your patients, and take care of all your family goals and objectives at the same time?

The challenge is making the most of the positives and minimizing the impact of the negatives. Part of my strategy as a financial advisor has been to help dentists find the multidisciplinary expertise they need. Dentists tend to work independently, which can isolate them

---

1 Guay, Albert, Matthew Warren, Rebecca Starkel, Marko Vujicic. "A Proposed Classification of Dental Group Practices." Research Brief. Health Policy Institute, American Dental Association (February 2014).

from their peers and other business owners. If that's you, you will encounter problems from time to time that you don't know how to solve. I can put you in touch with trustworthy people to assist in such specialties as estate and transition planning.

You will need to build a team of attorneys, accountants, business brokers, architects and designers, lenders, and others. My role is to help coordinate everybody's activities so that you have a good chance of being successful. Once your practice is running successfully, it's much easier to fully fund a 401(k) plan and other investments.

Nearly a decade ago, Linda Miles and I launched the Dental Business Network to ensure the business success of dentists. We help dentists weigh their priorities and find the very best leaders in their disciplines to help them become successful. If I don't have a particular expertise, I can point to people who do.

THE FUNDAMENTAL QUESTIONS

Here are a few revealing questions to ask yourself before we begin:

- Do I have a business plan for my practice that fully supports my personal financial plan and goals?

- Does my practice produce enough income so that I can live the way I want and also save enough for retirement, get out of debt, and put my kids through college?

- If I had to sell my practice tomorrow, do I know what it's worth?

- If I died tomorrow, would my practice survive?

If you answered no to any of these questions, you are not alone. Most dentists operate their dental practice without a formal business plan and don't have any idea what their practice is worth today.

You need to analyze your path. Retirement may not be this year, but decisions you make now influence your ability to achieve personal financial goals in the long term. For most dentists, it will take a tremendous amount of effort to align your resources toward success. Additionally, at some point, you will need to transition your practice. This process involves identifying somebody to take over the business who will pay you what it is worth at the right time to provide enough money for a dignified retirement.

That will not happen spontaneously. It will take some work and require help. In the pages ahead, I will identify the main issues you will need to address for a better outcome. The most important thing is to start *now*.

FINANCIAL FLOSSING

Each time I go to the dentist's office, the hygienist tells me about the importance of fluoride and brushing and flossing. Many people take that advice—but often, they soon are back to their old habits. It's not that patients don't know about healthy habits, but they just get distracted. Then along come the painful consequences.

The key is to figure out what you want early enough to start working on it consistently. In other words, you need to commit to a schedule of regular financial checkups. Cavities may not manifest as a patient's toothache today, but they will not get smaller on their own. If you don't deal with your financial problems today, you could be in for a lot of pain—financially.

Perhaps at times you have told a patient, "Let's watch that tooth for a while to see how it goes." Why not fix it today? A financial problem, like a dental problem, will just get worse. It's best to attend to the daily care, get checkups, and deal proactively with whatever might arise.

It's the same way with your personal finances. The longer you wait, the less likely it is that you will have good financial health.

No matter where you are on the arc of your career, you need to figure out where you stand, where you want to go, and what's possible. Year by year, or at least decade by decade, you need to lay out what you need to do. That's true whether you are more successful than you thought you would be or less so.

And you need to start now. If you are not wealthy, it will take a solid twenty years of effort to accumulate the savings you need to retire comfortably. You will have to find a way to save now and grow your business so that you have a good chance of success over the long run. There's no "get rich quick" scheme. Nobody will pay you several million dollars for your dental office just because that is what you need to retire.

I can show you a way of looking at the problems and obstacles and opportunities so that you can make the right decisions that will lead to success. *I emphasize the importance of starting now.* If you are right out of dental school or working as an associate dentist, pay attention to what the doctors a generation in front of you have been doing right and doing wrong. That will help you to make smart decisions. You won't end up working years longer than you had intended and end up regretting your chosen profession.

PART ONE

DENTISTS: A BREED APART

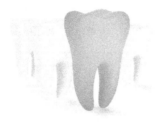

CHAPTER 1

WHY DENTISTS ARE SPECIAL

My father wanted to practice dentistry in his hometown, but he lived in rural Illinois in the early 1960s, where patients did not have the same money for dentistry that they do now.

My dad was a typical country doctor. Farmers and coal miners came in with toothaches, asked him to pull the tooth, and they would pay the fee. They would leave the office, and he wouldn't see them again. It made it difficult for the practice to be profitable.

At that time, there were a lot of new regulations and fees associated with dentistry. He hadn't anticipated those expenses that would further drain his ability to support his family and run a successful practice. In the early 1970s, high inflation and regulatory pressure outpaced his ability to raise fees and keep up with overhead. Meanwhile, the lab fees, price of gold, and supplies were also rising.

His profit margins collapsed, and he couldn't keep up with his household expenses and the debt. He ended up selling the practice and moving on to a more urban setting where more people could afford dentistry. He began to focus on being more productive as a dentist—seeing more patients, doing more work, and working more quickly so he could do more procedures.

The more patients he saw, the more money he would make. To perform the latest procedures, he needed to buy more equipment. To buy more equipment, he had to see more patients and raise his prices. That cycle of taking the profits from his business and reinvesting into the business was just starting for him back in the early 1970s.

Dad developed a new method of doing endodontics that was effective and quicker than what he had been taught in dental school. The old way was just too slow to allow him to see enough patients to be profitable. He ended up teaching his root canal techniques to thousands of dentists across the country.

Dad had to invent his own tools for his technique, so he started a second company as an inventor of hand pieces, endodontic files, clamps, and other products needed to do endodonticts. By the 1980s, my father was busily involved in dental product manufacturing and teaching.

Into the 1980s, he was in that cycle of manufacturing, teaching, and reinvesting into his business. That worked well until the recession of the early 1980s. Because general dentists couldn't afford to attend his seminars or buy his products, his business suffered. It survived, ultimately, but he had not been prepared for that interruption of cash flow, and for a time he lacked the money for the things he needed to do and for reinvesting in the business.

FIRST LESSONS

My parents' dental business was their "golden child." In the early 1980s, they didn't have the money to reinvest in the business and pay all the bills. There wasn't enough money for me to go to college, so I had to work my way through school. The "golden child" got the money that I might have used for tuition.

I tried to go to college on my own and then decided to join the navy, enlisting as a teenager. My college education was paid through the GI Bill. I persevered and soon became a commissioned nuclear submarine officer with an undergraduate degree in mechanical engineering from the University of Washington in Seattle, and I later did my master of science degree in operations research in Monterey in the late 1990s.

In the navy, I learned two highly valuable things. To serve on a nuclear submarine, you have to be able to operate the nuclear reactor and be an engineer. It was crucial to always have a plan in place for survival at sea, in case something went wrong. Every compartment of a submarine, even the boat's restroom or head, has two doors so that if a fire breaks out, escape is possible. No matter what happens, there is a backup plan in place.

In graduate school, I learned operations research, which applies mathematics to operational situations. I studied statistics, math and computer simulations to figure out the smartest possible way to use limited resources to get the best outcome. Academically, I became an efficiency expert.

In dentistry, I believe it comes down to this: The elements that explain most of the differences in doctors' income are marketing, new patient flow, the scheduling of a day's procedures, the pricing of the work, the mix of clinical procedures, and overhead control.

Ten years ago, when I was 38 years old, I had put in 20 years in the navy and was eligible for retirement as a lieutenant commander. I was a young man, relatively, and I needed to find something else to do. Many of my clients ask me why I never tried to become a dentist like my dad, but I have never felt that I had the steady hands required for that work.

I always admired dentists such as my father, though. It troubled me that he was a really smart, innovative, hardworking professional and business owner, and yet he was unable to achieve some universal financial planning goals, like having the money for his son to attend a university. He thought he would be able to pay it out of the cash flow of his business. But as I was about to graduate from high school, a recession hit. He didn't have the current income or the money set aside.

Later, when I decided to get into financial planning, I recalled this troubling memory and thought, "Maybe I could work with dentists to make sure they never have to have an awkward conversation with their children explaining why they don't have the money for college."

That was what motivated me. My father might have a different recollection, but in my mind, he did not plan well. I cannot say that I know what he could have done differently, and he did not have anybody like me in his corner trying to nudge him in a way that would work out. He was trying to figure out what to do on his own, without expert advice on making better long-term choices. He was busy solving the problem of the day.

Mostly, he succeeded. But from a planning perspective, he didn't put everything in place. He had a lot of income but not wealth. A dentist might be generating collections of $500,000 to $1.5 million annually, but the owner may not be on solid financial footing.

THE ABILITY TO BUILD EQUITY

From the perspective of many financial planners, dentists are often grouped with physicians, but they are really quite different. For one thing, the majority of dentists are self-employed. They own, or are partial owners of, their practice. Dentists tend to be the sole health-care provider in the business, whereas many physicians are in a group practice. A typical dental practice employs hygienists, assistants, and a front desk team.

Business owners can control both their revenue and their taxable profit. From a planning perspective, a general dentist in a strip mall has many more levers to play with than an employee physician earning a salary, 401(k), and health insurance, with no real control over the direction of the practice. For employed clients, a financial planner usually limits advice to minimize taxes and risks, develop a budget, and suggest investments. In assisting a business owner, however, an advisor can work on various levels to achieve financial goals.

Dentists tend to have significant equity in the business. It's common for a general dentistry practice to be worth 60 to 80 percent of what the office collects in a year, whereas a physician's practice with similar cash flow is usually worth significantly less.

In short, dentists are different not only in that they control their income, but also because they can build equity in a business that can be liquidated when the doctor is ready to retire.

GOAL PURSUIT: THE QUEST FOR SUCCESS

Today's dentists have plenty of opportunities to learn from the challenges of yesterday so they can seize a better tomorrow. Doctors have a lot of people who are relying on them—their patients, their staffs, their friends and families, and the charities they support. Much rides on the dentist's success, both in the short and long term. It's important that they set themselves up to succeed efficiently and without stress.

Dentists must embrace the importance of planning and acting early. This should not be an afterthought. They need to begin with the end in mind and understand where they are on their career arc and the milestones of progress to the next level. There are warning signs along the way that they should heed, and there are opportunities. They need a way of benchmarking their progress so that they don't get discouraged or overconfident.

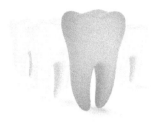

CHAPTER 2

WHEN BUSINESS GETS PERSONAL

" **P**ay yourself first" is an adage of financial planning, but it is hard for dentists to do that when they are typically the ones who get paid last.

They pay their staff, landlord, business banker, computer guy, supplier, and vendors first. If there's any money left over, then the dentist might get paid. At the end of the day, it feels nearly impossible to save any money.

So what's the doctor to do? Cut back on personal spending at the house in order to save money? Give up Starbucks, take cheaper vacations, and buy a less expensive car as a way of saving money for the future? Sometimes this strategy works, sometimes it doesn't.

It's analogous to going on a new diet. It doesn't feel comfortable. They have grown accustomed to the house and neighborhood, they like their cars and vacations, and they are happy with their children's schools and with their chosen charities. Any suggestion to change these habits will meet with resistance. Even if the doctor wants to cut back, the spouse and children may push back, and that in itself is stressful. The doctor wants to keep up with classmates from dental school who are taking fine vacations.

So there's a lot of pressure to maintain lifestyle expenses. Resistance to change is common. We're comfortable with what we have now, and we may fail to plan for the comfort we will need later. It's procrastination—we all think it will be easier to save money next year when we're making more.

Like most financial planners, I have put my clients on a financial diet, but eventually they rebel. I'll get a call from a client who says, "Guess what, I just bought a new boat," or "We just got back from Las Vegas." It's difficult to change money habits; psychologically, we undermine ourselves.

But why cut back? There's a better way for dentists to pursue goals. Business owners have unique opportunities to create the needed cash flow.

Let's say the doctor's personal budget to support the family lifestyle comes to $10,000 a month or $120,000 a year. Add to that insurance—health insurance, liability insurance, disability insurance, life insurance—costing $20,000 a year. A mortgage and some student loan debt add $40,000 annually, and the array of various taxes can amount to $60,000 a year. That all adds up to $240,000 a year.

Somebody in this situation may need to be saving about 20 percent of his or her income for long-term goals, such as retirement and college. So if he's consuming $240,000 a year, he needs to be saving about $48,000 a year. That raises the total to $288,000 a year.

Assume a dental practice has overhead that is 60 percent of collections. That means the doctor needs $720,000 in collections in order to have that $288,000 available each year for lifestyle expenses and investments. If annual collections are $700,000 a year and the doctor needs to collect $720,000 a year, it's much easier for the doctor to figure out a way to collect an extra $20,000 a year than to try to reduce a personal budget by the same amount.

That's the prevailing theme of this book—doctors' business decisions should support their personal reality and goal pursuit. By understanding their personal financial situation, they can set their business goals to achieve their personal ones.

With the problem framed from this perspective, it may become easier to figure production goals for the dental office. The doctor will know how much money is needed at home and how much must be saved each year. This approach is simpler and leaves dentists happier than if they try to cut back by skipping Starbucks.

Dentists often look at their professional goals without connecting them to their personal goals. Many times, doctors will buy new equipment without having any idea of how that equipment purchase will improve the cash flow of their business. They will remodel their offices or begin a marketing plan without knowing what the return on investment must be, and many times they won't even truly understand how much money their practice must generate to meet their personal financial goals.

Business and personal finances are connected, so personal and business plans should be as well. If it's the doctor's personal goal to work to age 75, then he or she must save much less money than would be required to retire at age 55. Conversely, a doctor who intends to retire at 55 must work much harder and make much more money than somebody choosing to work 20 years longer. The doctor needs to develop a plan to support whatever the goal might be and then move forward with confidence.

Sometimes, it comes down to some tough questions:

- What is the doctor willing to do to control personal consumption?

- What is the doctor willing to do professionally to earn more money?

- How will the doctor fill the gap between what's currently available and what is needed?

THE WHEEL OF PRIORITIES

Practice operation affects cash flow, and since the doctor gets paid last, anything that improves that cash flow will improve the doctor's income. A lot of factors influence that cash flow, including location of the practice, procedures performed in the office, the insurance carriers, scheduling, expenses, staffing, technology, and the use of debt.

A desired improvement in cash flow and revenue calls for a close look at the dental practice's metrics. For example, clinical supplies are historically benchmarked at 6 percent of collections. If the supply cost is higher, say 10 percent, then we have identified an area for potential improvement. The doctor could also look at the cost of staff, typically benchmarked at 20 percent of collections—although, pragmatically, it is difficult to cut staff salaries. Also, if accounts receivable extend beyond two weeks, that's probably a place to improve profitability.

The current value of a practice is correlated to current collections. If the practice collects more money, and other factors are constant, then the owner's net discretionary income increases and the practice is worth more.

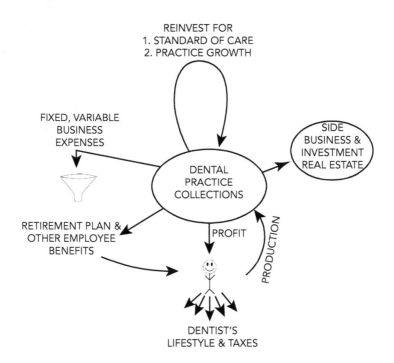

Wheel of Priorities: The dentist provides care and directs all aspects of the dental practice. The dental practice generates collections from dentistry. Starting on the left side of the diagram: collections can be consumed by fixed and variable expenses; they can be reinvested in the dental practice to improve the "standard of care" or for practice growth; collections may be moved over to a side business, other investments, or real estate; collections may be invested in a retirement plan or other employee benefits. Anything left is available for the dentist's lifestyle or taxes.

The doctor is at the center of a Wheel of Priorities. The doctor chooses how to live, when to retire, and how to run the practice. The doctor is solely responsible for whatever happens and, therefore, must understand what the stakes are and what needs to be done to make better decisions today.

Lifestyle affects long-term financial goals, determining how much money the doctor must save and how long it will be until retirement. Those long-term financial goals should, in turn, affect the business plan. The business should rise to the challenge of meeting the lifestyle goals of the doctor, as well as such goals as buying a house or saving for college or for retirement.

With harmony between lifestyle and business operations, the doctor may have more enthusiasm about his or her career and role as a leader at home, in the community, and within the practice.

How doctors operate their business will directly affect their home life and ability to secure a financial future. It's important that they understand what they want out of life and then make their business achieve that.

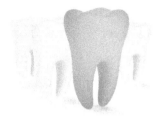

CHAPTER 3

FINANCIAL MALOCCLUSION

It takes brains and hard work to become a dentist. Unfortunately, because of the years of education required, few dentists are in a position to save money in their early 20s, when it would most benefit them.

Once they graduate, they can earn significant income, although less than an experienced dentist can earn. Many have huge college student loans and dental school debts, perhaps $100,000 to $300,000.

And because they have been in school for so long, life often moves very quickly when they graduate, including marriage, families, and home purchases. So any money that's coming in is getting diverted to life expenses and student loans. Little money remains to save, regardless of the amount of income. Most don't really start saving any money until their mid-30s, which makes it difficult to become wealthy, even with a six-figure income.

I have spoken to doctors in their 50s who aren't even close to having the amount of money that they will need. Many have lived paycheck to paycheck and never got around to putting money away on a systematic basis. It breaks my heart to talk to doctors in their 50s who can't afford to send their children to college or doctors who don't have significant money in a 401(k) plan. Most likely, such doctors will be working well into their 70s to accumulate enough money for a decent retirement.

It happens frequently, and I'm trying to fix this fact by offering some smarter options and getting doctors to start earlier. They may be in their 40s and 50s by the time they are through school, have their debts at a manageable level, and are running a moderately successful practice. Now they really need to turn it up and accumulate the money they will need to pull it off. For both the new doctor and the seasoned one, there is hope and a path to success.

Don't get me wrong; it takes hard work. The focus needs to be on achieving personal goals, not on what one's peers believe is best. Each year needs to be a step forward, making the most of opportunities and avoiding the pitfalls that get so many people off track.

COMPETING OBJECTIVES

One of the biggest obstacles that dentists face early in their careers is what to pay first. They ask questions such as these:

- Should I be making extra mortgage payments?

- Should I be investing money into my own practice?

- Should I pay for my child's education?

- Should I be focusing on my retirement accounts?

Making long-view financial decisions can be hard with all the pressures that doctors face right out of school, but it is essential for a successful retirement. The biggest asset is time. The earlier they start, the easier it is to manage their behavior as investors, to accumulate the money that they need, and to build good financial habits.

I meet people who have never thought about these ideas until they are almost ready to retire, and there is little that I can do. I take what they bring me and make the best of it. Certainly, a younger doctor will be much better off by applying some of these principles earlier.

With so many competing objectives, it is important to prioritize what is important. If the doctor places high value in a private education for his or her children, then we have to find the money to afford it. The way to do that is by building a business that supports the doctor's desired lifestyle.

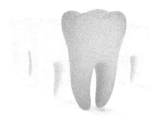

CHAPTER 4

POWER PLANNING

Doctors need a way to transform excess profits from their business into something that can meet whatever personal goals they have.

With focus, it generally takes 20 or 30 years to accumulate sufficient wealth to retire. Because of the many years of education needed, dentists get a late start, and it takes time to build a bustling practice. And by age 60, they often slow down or start to burn out. So there's a relatively brief window of time to accumulate the wealth needed to retire.

Their challenge is very different from that of many others, who start working and saving while in their early 20s. Maybe those others are making less money, but they are saving it over a longer period. They have a much better shot of maintaining their lifestyle in retirement than does somebody who is making $200,000 a year for fewer years. The math on that is clear.

A FALSE SENSE OF SECURITY

Many dentists underestimate the amount of money that they should be saving. They haven't calculated their required annual savings rate to achieve their financial independence goals.

They need to ask themselves these questions:

- If I were going to retire at age 65, how much money would I need?

- How much money do I need to save each year to achieve that goal?

- Am I saving that much?

Many times, doctors get complacent, because they are saving money in a SIMPLE IRA, or they are putting money into their 401(k) plan, but they may not really be mathematically on track to accumulate sufficient money in their most productive years. In addition, they might have other major expenses that interrupt their ability to save for their retirement. It might be their children's education. It might be a larger home. It might be reinvestment into their practice.

They need to have a clear picture of their net worth, their assets and liabilities, and how much income they can expect or would hope to have each year. They also need a clear household and business budget and the ability to earn enough to meet those needs while saving according to their financial plan.

Out of that, they need to develop a plan for just how much to save and how to invest it. They also need to understand what they can expect from investment performance—both in the short run with regard to volatility, and in the long run with regard to growth. Success doesn't mean getting the expected historical investment performance or always outdoing what the average investor gets.

SETTING GOALS FOR A ROBUST PLAN

Goal setting is an essential step for any doctor, and a CERTIFIED FINANCIAL PLANNER™ Professional should be helping to build a robust financial plan.

Many times, doctors think that they are setting goals, but when asked about it, they get fuzzy and it is obvious they are winging it. The doctor must emotionally own and commit to goals. They must be able to articulate what they want to happen and then set to work to make it happen.

As a financial planner, I'm in the goal pursuit and achievement business. The doctors tell me what they want to achieve, and I show them how to get it in the most efficient and stress-free way possible. For example: if the goal is retirement, we must explore what that means. To some, it means not working at all and living on a golf course; others want to start a second career outside of dentistry.

After the goals are identified, it gets much easier to quantify them and figure out how much money it will take to meet those goals with a margin of safety. Working backward from there, we can figure the amount of savings needed and how investments should be managed to support the goals with a very high probability of reaching them.

Financial goals must be specific and have an emotional commitment behind them. When I started as a planner, people would tell me, "Well, when I'm 65, what I want is $100,000 a year coming in, and I don't want to have to work for it. I want enough money to be able to do that."

A lot of times, that seems like a very specific goal. But it can be difficult for people to commit to that, because something always comes up. Perhaps they want a boat, or they want to remodel the office, or they want to put their kids in a different private school, or they want a new car, or they want an exotic vacation.

Things like that tend to wreck financial plans. There is no emotional commitment to just being able to retire at 65 and having money coming in. A better goal might be to have $100,000 a year coming in, so that the client and spouse have the time to relax and enjoy the fruits of their labor and walk their dogs along the beach at sunset.

Financial independence, eliminating student loan debt, getting the house paid off, getting the business paid off, and providing for their children's education are the most common goals that I help dentists achieve. Growing the dental practice is another common goal. Many doctors want to have a million-dollar practice, which means a practice that generates a million dollars in collections each year. That's a tangible goal. For some, legacy is important; they want to be in a position to leave money to the charities and the people that they care about and still maintain their lifestyle. Those can be emotionally driven goals, and working toward achieving them is fun for both the client and for me.

FOCUSING ON FINANCIAL INDEPENDENCE

The cornerstone of every financial plan that I have ever written has been the early achievement of financial independence. For me, a client's financial independence requires enough wealth to maintain their current lifestyle, do the things that they want to do, take care of the people that they want to take care of, and have 100 percent ownership of their time without having to work for a paycheck. For many people, this is a goal to achieve as soon as possible. It does not necessarily mean that they will stop doing dentistry. But they want to know that they could.

There are many important variables that every dentist needs to consider to get to financial independence.

ANNUAL SAVINGS RATE

Often, doctors start out their working life without money. They might have a decent paycheck, but the net worth, assets minus liabilities, is zero, or it may be negative if they have significant student loan or mortgage or car or credit card debt. They have to get from that zero point to having millions of dollars.

The primary variable, at least for the first 10 to 20 years of a doctor's adult working life, will be the doctor's ability to consistently save money on an annual basis. I often see a gap between the amount of money that clients mathematically need to save to achieve the goal and what they are willing to commit toward it. The savings rate for a financial plan must be feasible. Either they save the required amount, or they need to change the goal.

TIME HORIZON

The biggest thing that affects the required annual savings rate is *how much time is available* to save. Starting from zero, there's a major difference in the savings rate needed to retire in 20 years compared with 10 or 15 years. It takes time for investments to grow.

It's important to start early, but goals don't change just because of a late start. Given that the retirement date is generally fixed, the thing to focus on is the savings rate. The doctor must find the money to achieve the goal. I'm a supply-side CERTIFIED FINANCIAL PLANNER™ Professional. I try to look at the money that's moving through the dental practice as a tool to improve the client's saving rate.

In a robust financial plan, common obstacles won't cause failure. If somebody intends to retire at age 55, then they need a resilient financial plan. To retire sooner requires more money in one's investment accounts. Social Security benefits and Medicare don't kick in for people who are retiring early. In general, Social Security is not available for people who are younger than 62. Medicare does not begin to provide health benefits until age 65. Initially without Social Security, a retired dentist will have to be prepared to spend accumulated assets more quickly until benefits begin.

BUDGETING FOR RETIREMENT LIFESTYLE

It's difficult for doctors to estimate how much money they will want when they are 65 or 75 or 80 years old. Some people spend less than before they retired, but others need more to pay for health insurance that is no longer pre-tax or to do the traveling for which they finally have time.

I have found that it is just not palatable for most doctors to significantly cut back on the lifestyle that they have grown accustomed to over their adult working lives. They are just not going to move out of their houses to a cheaper apartment. They are not going to get rid of the Cadillac and drive a Chevrolet. They are not going to find new friends in a region with a lower cost of living.

The most critical period of retirement is the five years before the doctor retires and the five years afterward. After that, things tend to steady out. People develop new habits. But this is the point when the doctors probably have the biggest nest egg that they have ever had, and mistakes could jeopardize everything that they have worked toward.

REAL INVESTMENT RETURN AFTER INFLATION AND TAXES

It is a good indication that a financial plan is robust if it works with historically conservative growth rates on investments. If the plan only seems to work during a bull stock market, or if the interest rates that savers receive on bonds or bank CDs must remain high to succeed, then it is probably time to rethink one's assumptions.

It's also important to anticipate the taxes for each investment. There's a big difference between the tax treatment of a treasury bond, the tax treatment of a Roth IRA, the tax treatment on the sale of a business, and the tax treatment on the sale of a personal residence.

The taxation when liquidating investments makes a big difference in how much money will be available for retirement income. The dental office is a significant asset for many dentists, so it's important to know its value and to have a game plan for getting the value out of that dental office for retirement. I advise doctors to be conservative and consider every angle in forecasting what the practice will be worth in 10 or 20 years. They need to temper expectations about how much somebody will be willing to pay and the terms.

ASSET ALLOCATION OF INVESTMENTS

No matter what investment we are talking about, the goal is to potentially maximize return for a given risk or to minimize risk for a given expected total return.

I have seen doctors either investing too conservatively to achieve their financial goals or trying to catch up and investing too aggressively for their situation. I help them to take a step back and assess their options from a goal achievement point of view. Retirement is extremely expensive if a doctor chooses to maintain a current lifestyle. Typically, there's a benchmark, such as about $2 million in investments is needed in today's dollars to produce every $80,000 of retirement income. To maintain the accustomed lifestyle, a doctor retiring today typically would need $2 million to $4 million of liquid assets.

INFLATION

No one can afford to ignore the effects of inflation. If inflation is 3 percent annually over the next ten years, then doctors retiring a decade from now will need $2.7 million to $5.4 million. If they plan to retire 20 years from now, instead of needing $2 million to $4 million, they will need $3.6 million to $7.2 million.

These are scary numbers. Just like everything else that they have achieved in life, doctors have to start early and work on it over time to acquire the liquid assets needed to leave dentistry and maintain their lifestyle. It's not terribly hard to achieve this, but it does take focus and a long-term perspective.

POTENTIAL PASSIVE INCOME STREAMS

Sometimes, other money is available. Some clients have inheritances from their parents, existing annuity income, or pensions from a spouse or military pension and Social Security income. Sometimes, they have rental real estate, or they are renting their dental office or a second home that provides passive income.

If those sources are available, then they need to be incorporated into the financial plan, as they tend to reduce the amount of additional money needed for retirement—and that means less money to be saved every year before retirement.

Every strategy is unique. There are different variables, and sometimes goals can be achieved more easily by moving the levers in different ways. These variables work together to reach their goals as efficiently as possible.

PLANNING TO TRANSITION THE DENTAL PRACTICE

For most doctors, the sale of their business is the biggest liquidity event of their lifetimes. How they achieve that transition makes a big difference in how much money they will have and the retirement lifestyle they will enjoy.

The five years before the sale is an essential period for a successful transition plan. By this point, the dental office might be worth as much as a million dollars. The planning of that transition—the sale of the business, how it is done and when, the taxation, and how the proceeds are reinvested—makes a huge difference in the success of a retirement plan. A doctor who is considering a transition offer without having first conducted a tax-sensitive analysis as part of a comprehensive financial plan has pretty much already lost the tax battle. In my experience, that means he or she will pay more tax than would have been necessary. We will take a close look at transition planning in chapter 12.

PLAN FOR THE WORST, HOPE FOR THE BEST

A robust financial plan needs to plan for the worst, because sometimes bad things happen. It can be hard to think about contingencies, but wishful thinking simply won't suffice for planning.

What happens, for example, if the doctor suddenly dies? The thought of that terrible hypothetical event triggers a whole series of questions that a financial plan must be ready to withstand:

- Is there enough money to maintain the family's accustomed lifestyle?

- Can the family afford to stay in their home?

- How will the practice be sold?

- What's the value of the business six months after the doctor dies?

- Will the equity in the practice be enough to cover the business debts?

- Who will take care of the payroll if the doctor passes away prematurely?

Without a financial planning process, few of these issues are likely to be addressed. In my experience, the spouse is never in a position to take over the operations of the dental practice and sell it for top dollar immediately after the dentist's death. So planning for that worst-case scenario is extremely important.

Permanent disability is another catastrophic contingency that people seldom address. Disability insurance must have an own-occupation definition of disability, the maximum monthly benefit, and provide disability claim benefits for the dentist's working career. Those doctors who cannot get such coverage must find other strategies to deal with the risk of disability. Even when the doctor returns to work, the practice's financial situation probably will be very different. So an in-depth look at what would happen in these common scenarios is important. Things must be in place *before* there's a crisis.

DEALING WITH DEBT

Debt is a big roadblock to retirement. Whether it's a house mortgage or a business loan, debt must be rectified to attain financial independence. Many financial planners say the most important thing to do is to focus first on paying down the debt. But if dentists spend all of their time and funds paying off their educational loans, mortgages, and other debts exclusively, they will never get around to saving. I'll show in chapter 6 why repaying debts as quickly as possible actually might get in the way of becoming wealthy.

RIDING OUT THE HIGHS AND LOWS

Dentists, like other businesspeople, must contend with economic cycles. The business needs to be structured to take advantage of good times. On the flip side, when there's a severe recession, the practice needs to be flexible enough to survive and adapt. Dentists must ask themselves whether they have reserves in place to help pay all the bills.

A strong financial plan can also help take the emotion out of investing in the stock market. Without the right discipline, the doctors' own behavior and biases can pressure them into making bad decisions in both bull and bear markets. Swings in the markets will lead people to sell at low points and buy at high points, whittling down the gains needed for retirement. Simply put, the doctor's financial plan should address the impact of a future bear market on the pursuit of goals.

GROWING PAINS

Many dentists are golden-handed clinicians but ham-fisted business owners. Many ignore key business metrics as long as the schedule is full. They are sometimes quite happy with what they are doing, and they feel that they couldn't make more money, even if they needed to do so. They must understand that their ability to grow the practice will make a tremendous difference not only in their lifestyle when they are working but also in their ability to save money for retirement and ultimately in the value of the dental practice when they get ready to sell.

HAVING AN EXIT STRATEGY

Some doctors will have a date set in stone. Finding a buyer is many times problematic; sometimes it takes several years to find a buyer, who then backs out. Or maybe the buyer wants to buy the practice right now, and they don't want to wait until your ideal date. The dental practice is an illiquid investment, and efficiently monetizing that investment on the doctor's time line is oftentimes a major obstacle. The senior or selling dentist's financial plan must have the flexibility to change the price, the date, or the terms of the deal so that everybody is happy.

GETTING BUY-IN

Many senior doctors bring on associate dentists to do the work in the practice but don't want to provide an equity stake for the junior doctor, for many reasons. Sometimes it's a control issue; sometimes it's a money issue. If an associate who is counted on to generate additional income leaves, there will be a reduction in daily production and additional costs for finding a new doctor to fill the associate's shoes. If the doctor leaves abruptly, the senior doctor may now inherit all of the associate's work, too.

Managing the associate dentist's expectations and still meeting financial objectives can be challenging. Having strong financial and business plans in place and reviewing them on an annual basis helps to alleviate much of the stress for both parties.

LEARNING AND TAKING ACTION

I often tell my clients that they must become financially literate. Many dentists throw themselves into running their businesses without having any business experience or fundamental knowledge as to how to run a business.

Many times, they are the only business owner in the family, and they do a lot of things by trial and error. They have no time to learn some of the basics of money, such as cash flow, the time value of money, or debt payment. As the business environment changes, dentists need someone to help them keep up. They cannot simply keep doing things the same way.

Sometimes, when I speak to doctors about implementing basic strategies to save profits while they are generating a lot of revenue, they will decline because they are "too busy." This response is a red flag to me, a signal of procrastination. Procrastination is one of the worst enemies of a financial plan. It can cost years of progress and earnings. It's much better to just get on with it without delay.

THE WORST OBSTACLE OF ALL

Many times, doctors will think, "I'm making $200,000 a year, I'm putting money in my 401(k) and following the rules, and I should be fine." And they get to their mid-50s, and their financial advisor has to explain that there's no way they can retire in ten years, because they aren't wealthy.

It can be tragic. They just deny that there's a need to do any planning or that planning cannot help them. They see no problem and figure they don't need to do anything. It happens more than you would think. When I'm talking to a doctor and that's the issue, there's little that I can do to help. How can we talk about a change if the doctor doesn't believe that anything needs to be changed? It's sad, and I know how the story will end. The math on that is very clear.

POST-RETIREMENT OBSTACLES

Once a doctor has overcome the obstacles of getting to retirement, there is another set of challenges during retirement.

Often, retirees have no idea what to do with their time. It may sound silly, but failure to effectively set goals before retiring could lead to overspending in the years to come. Having a plan can make all the difference.

Several of the obstacles are the same as before retirement—inflation, debt, personal budgeting. The retiree must have enough liquid assets to handle day-to-day expenses and contingencies such as a home's new roof. How much money might be expected from Social Security or perhaps a pension? What will be sold and when? How will the doctor pay basic expenses and then variable expenses throughout a 30-year retirement? It takes a lot of thought and planning. Having $4 million in an investment account does not mean the cash flow will work.

Older people face more health-care issues. They may have a long-term-care need, whether at home or in a facility. Many times, long-term-care insurance covers these things. Sometimes it doesn't and must be paid out of pocket. All these things tend to burn up cash, and there should be enough money in the doctor's financial plan to come up with, conservatively, $100,000 for unexpected bills.

Similarly, estate planning will be more important than ever before. Assets must be left to a surviving spouse or children in a protected manner. Many times, the doctor will have accumulated several million dollars, more than enough. He or she may end up leaving a few million dollars to a spouse or to children who have never managed money. Unprotected, the money is at the mercy of the recipients' financial whims and could be lost to creditors or to a divorce claim. The doctor's years of hard work can be annihilated quickly. With just a little more planning, the doctor could have done a much better job of taking care of the family.

Lastly, there's a risk that most dentists don't even consider, and it can come back to bite them. Let's say the doctor sells the practice to a junior associate and has an agreement whereby the purchaser pays $5,000 a month over five years. If that junior doctor gets in financial trouble, that "guaranteed" money may be tied up for a long time—or disappear altogether.

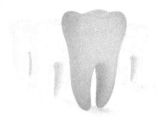

CHAPTER 5

STRATEGY FOR SUCCESS

The basic strategy to accumulate money is really quite simple. First, stop being an associate dentist employee and startup or purchase a dental practice. Grow the practice to the point where it provides a decent standard of living, pays all the household bills, puts money into an emergency fund, and reduces any consumer debt. Sounds easy, right?

Once a practice reaches that state of self-sufficiency, it becomes a financial tool that provides for the future of the doctor's family. It is important to measure progress and reevaluate goals annually, considering the financial purpose of the practice. If the dentist knows when he or she will retire and is clear about the desired lifestyle, it's easy to calculate the sum needed—and how much to save each year.

Doctors often are shell-shocked when they realize they may need to save between $50,000 to $80,000 each and every year. Doctors in their mid-30s might find it stressful to anticipate saving that much each year, but it can be necessary in order to retire by the target date with the desired standard of living.

Few doctors use the process of reverse engineering to figure out what they need to accomplish day by day to reach success. Usually, they work as hard and smart as they can and then try to make do with what comes out. It's important to reevaluate the practice and its business strategy. If the business is not generating enough money, then the doctor must decisively reinvest in it so the practice can grow to the point where it can easily fund lifestyle expenses, repay debt, and save for various goals.

When the business is producing the required cash flow, it's time to set up a savings plan and investment program to achieve those goals. The doctor can put money into a retirement account or a college account month after month and invest it wisely. With the necessary amount set aside, the doctor can spend the rest pretty much as desired.

PROTECTIVE MEASURES

Once achieved, wealth must be safeguarded. The doctor should have enough cash in the business to survive, make payroll, and pay creditors without new money coming in for some period. Or if something were to malfunction, the doctor would be able to write a big check right away without any trouble. That emergency fund probably should be at least enough to cover a month's payroll, for starters.

Business owners also must understand the need for access to capital. They should have a good relationship with their business banker, so that if they need a large chunk of money for expansion, for training, for a new piece of equipment, or for a new opportunity, they can borrow it without raiding their personal checking account.

Another important protective stance is having a disability plan. Doctors need to have a plan to not just cover their own personal expenses but also to put the dental practice in a position where it could survive any kind of disability or incapacity of the doctor. I know of one doctor who needed hand surgery that kept him from dentistry for six months. He had personal disability insurance for that period, but he needed to pay the staff members so they would still be there when he reopened the doors. He ended up burning through a tremendous amount of his personal money just to keep his office from closing.

A business succession plan is essential. The doctor must arrange powers of attorney so that family and key members of the staff can perform basic functions, such as paying bills, hiring or firing, and negotiating with lenders. If the doctor were to be permanently disabled, who would be able to step in quickly to begin selling the practice, if that's what it comes down to, or shrinking the business so that it can survive for an extended time? If that person must figure out payroll and other duties, would he or she have contact information for all the vendors, the CPA, the attorney, and others? Where is that information kept? Generally, it's in the doctor's head. A little bit of planning now can save a lot of trouble in the future.

If it's a group practice and there's a junior associate, is there anything in the employment contract or business agreement or a buy-sell agreement that would require that associate to provide for the practice if the senior doctor were injured? Is there an operations plan for scheduling if the doctor is out for surgery for a few weeks?

A lot of dental offices do not incorporate a maternity plan into the business. If the doctor had a baby, who would take care of the patients during the maternity period? Will she really be able to come right back at the same pace following the birth of the child?

Whether it's disability or a pregnancy, such matters are better addressed. Mature million-dollar businesses must find a way to survive the common circumstance when the doctor will be out for a while.

Doctors also must attend to the basics of asset protection—deliberately positioning key assets and setting up entities and procedures so that if the doctor is sued, or if the business fails, future creditors will be limited in how much they could get. Without planning, doctors in such a situation could lose everything or face garnishment of future earnings. It's a risk that needs to be addressed.

THE RIGHT EXIT STRATEGY

Even if the doctor has no intention of selling the practice for several decades, it's never too early to consider the exit strategy. Preparation helps to protect one's interests. Doctors should ask themselves this: Given what I know now, how would I prefer to leave or transition the practice? What route is most comfortable for me?

For the practice owner there are two primary considerations: What is the practice worth, and how is the dentist likely to exit the profession? Will the practice be sold after the doctor dies, be passed on to heirs, or be sold to a third party beforehand? The doctor doesn't need to know exactly what will happen but should have a preference in mind. That preference can become part of the business planning so that the doctor can make the most of the opportunity when it comes up.

If the doctor expects to retire in a few years, it's time to consider the best positioning to make the most of the opportunity. Can the doctor grow the practice? Pay off debt? Upgrade equipment? What could he or she be doing to maximize the business value?

I often see doctors getting older and tired and hitting a point where they want to retire. It's then that they look around and start asking questions. "What's my dental practice worth, and who will pay me for it?" If that's their strategy, they almost certainly will not get top dollar for the dental practice, and they may pay more in taxes and fees than they otherwise would have with just a little bit of planning.

Many things must be accomplished. The practice must be valued, the equipment must be valued, and if the building will be sold, too, then that also must be valued. A buyer needs to be identified. Sometimes several buyers must be identified, because buyers sometimes back out at the last minute, and lost time is lost money. All these efforts must be coordinated with the doctor's CERTIFIED FINANCIAL PLANNER™ Professional, certified public accountant, attorney, and a dental practice broker to identify the best price and terms.

Once the doctor has the check in hand, and once taxes, debts, and fees have been paid, it's time to reinvest the money so that it can grow in accordance with the doctor's financial plan.

FUNDAMENTAL QUESTIONS

Here are some examples of basic questions that I ask doctors, and many times their answers indicate that they still have a significant amount of work to do and a lot of considerations to think through.

- What would be the most productive use of your money? Should you put it back into the business, into a 401(k), pay off debt, or take your spouse on a vacation?

- What is your strategy to minimize taxes? For most of my dentists, taxes are the biggest expense—more than their mortgage and more than living expenses. So anything that reduces taxes, year after year, makes a huge difference in the amount of money that they can save.

- How are you managing cash flow? How do you prioritize everything in your business and your personal life so that you are consistently making a good call?

- How do you anticipate and prepare for major issues that might arise? All sorts of things can throw a wrench in a doctor's plans, from recession to divorce to disability to a partnership breaking up. Sound basic planning can minimize the damage. It's like a fire drill: when that alarm bell rings, you will remain calm and avoid panic.

- What are reasonable goals with regard to expanding the dental practice? How much money should you make, and could you make, from the dental office?

- How are you preparing for the transition of the dental practice?

- What have you done to restructure your business and personal debt?

Frankly, it's clear that a lot of dentists have not thought about these things, and nobody has ever asked them these questions before. In the next section, we will take a closer look at some of these matters.

PART TWO

FINANCIAL
HOUSEKEEPING

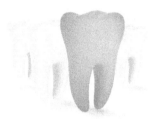

CHAPTER 6

THE DANCE OF DEBT

New dentists coming into the profession are often laden with debt. It's very common for a doctor to have student loans from their undergraduate degree as well as those incurred during dental school. The doctor's spouse might also have student loan debt, as well as a mortgage, car payments, and credit cards.

In order to get into the business of dentistry, it's likely that they are borrowing more than a half-million dollars more. When high-income doctors come in to see me the first time, they often have a negative net worth—their debts greatly outweigh their assets.

The net worth or balance sheet statement is like an equation. If you add a dollar on the asset side, that has exactly the same impact as paying back one dollar of debt. So on the face of it, many doctors feel that they should start saving later. They want to pay off some of their debts; it feels terribly stressful to be almost a million dollars in debt when patients and staff and family are depending on you.

NOT SO FAST

Many doctors, to their detriment, say: "Getting out of debt is my most important financial goal." They will use all of their income to try to get out of debt as quickly as possible because they would feel better, or because being debt-free is consistent with their personal money script and values.

However, if you are paying down a dollar of debt, that's a dollar that is not going into your investment accounts. It's a dollar that is not reinvesting in the growth of the dental practice. For most, the best-case scenario is that it would take about a decade to become debt-free. Some highly respected financial planners advocate this strategy. The rationale is that debt is a character flaw or a bad habit; it is such a financial drag and destroyer of wealth that one should shake off the debt first before beginning the accumulation of money. I disagree; I believe that a person's habits become their destiny. The habit of paying down and avoiding debt is not the same as the habit of saving and investing systematically.

Mathematically, the no-debt strategy makes it harder to become wealthy. The doctor ends up with significantly less money than would be available after paying off a little bit of debt year in and year out. It's important that doctors work on not just paying off debts but also on paying them off in a way that grows net worth fastest.

For example, the annual contribution into a retirement-type account is limited. So if the doctor has $50,000 available annually to either pay down debts or save for the future and decides to use this income year in and year out to pay down debt without putting it into a retirement account, this major opportunity is missed.

What will happen is this: Ten years later, the doctor will have no debt. Now, instead of having $50,000 available to save, the doctor might have $100,000 available to save, but the 401(k) plan bucket is still limited to about $53,000. The IRS sets contribution limits on how much money can go into a qualified plan.

So it's very important, when developing a strategy to get out of debt, that doctors take into account the impact of what they are giving away.

As I write this, interest rates are fairly low. For dentists who may need a loan, when rates are low it may make sense to accept a loan of several hundred thousand dollars at 4 or 5 percent interest over 10, 20 or 30 years and pay it off over time. Income required to accelerate debt repayment can be used for better purposes than quickly paying off a low-interest loan. If and when rates rise, this strategy may change.

The doctor needs to find the right mix of accumulating assets and reducing debt. On which side of the net worth statement, assets, or liabilities will the doctor's efforts be most productive? Investments that can produce a rate of return that exceed your borrowing cost will improve your net worth statement faster than just paying down debt. If you put $10,000 in an investment that can be expected to grow at 6 or 8 percent, that's better strategy over time than rapidly paying off a low-interest loan at 3 or 4 percent. That difference, the spread over many years, makes a huge difference in a doctor's net worth.

Please remember that we're trying to grow that net worth to the point that the doctor becomes wealthy. There are many wealthy people who have debt. It has nothing to do with character. There are many people who are not wealthy who have no debt, too.

Additionally, accounts like 401(k)s, IRAs, and Roth IRAs have statutory protections built in. If a doctor is sued or files for bankruptcy due to a business failure, those qualified assets are protected. If the goal is to pay off all the debts of the dental practice, and then that million-dollar dental practice goes out of business or is sued, the result is equity lost. There's no protection. And so putting money in a tax qualified investment, that is generally outside of your bankruptcy estate, may make more sense than paying off debt on an unprotected asset.

The other thing that's important to know is that by rapidly paying down loan principle, in general you are using after-tax dollars. After-tax dollars are expensive. We'll talk about that in chapter 10.

The doctor's balance sheet growth is significantly impacted because they have less time than the average worker to save and fully fund retirement. They get a late start, and they have the highest marginal tax rates relative to other people. So using those years to pay down debt severely impacts the doctor's peak net worth.

Another potential problem with repaying debt too rapidly is this: If you give, say, an extra $100,000 to your mortgage company, you can't get it back from the lender. You are reducing the balance but not your payment—and now you cannot use that $100,000 for some other opportunity or contingency. You cannot go to your mortgage lender and say, "I know I paid you this extra $100,000 when times were good a few years ago, but I'd like the money back."

Recall that the interest on the business debt is a deductible expense, but the principal repayment is generally not tax deductible. So if the business loan payment is $100,000 a year, and interest on that $10,000 a year, the doctor gets a $10,000 tax deduction. The remaining $90,000 principal payment is not deductible. CPAs refer to this $90,000 as phantom income.

The strategy that most CPAs will help you with is to depreciate assets over time so that you have the depreciation benefit to offset that payment of principal to the bank. It's the same way with business equipment, where the interest is a deductible expense but the principal repayment of the loan is an after-tax expense.

Similarly, on loans for leasehold improvements, outlays can be offset by proper amortization of the leasehold improvement in accordance with IRS rules. Dentists should work with tax professionals to determine the right strategy for their situation.

LOANS WITH STRINGS ATTACHED

Doctors need to understand that business debt almost always requires the acceptance of a personal guarantee. This is the banking industry standard because the corporation borrowing the money is dependent on the borrower/dentist to generate the collections that will repay the loan. Many times, doctors do not understand or consider the asset protection implications of a practice loan. The definition of personal guarantee will vary by lender, which means you should ask a lot of questions, but generally it means that liquid nonretirement assets controlled by the borrower (bank and brokerage accounts) will be claimed by the lender if the borrower defaults.

Lenders control risk in various ways. One way is by charging higher interest rates, but they also may keep the interest rate lower by covering their risk in other ways. Personal guarantees are a way for the lender to minimize the risk of default. Borrowers should consider the asset protection and broader financial planning ramifications of this type of loan. Many times, when doctors are considering one loan over another, they are just looking at the monthly payment or interest rate and are not considering the implications of a business loan default on their personal finances.

Additionally, most business lenders will require the bank assignment of personal life insurance or personal disability insurance. These premiums on life insurance policies are almost always after-tax expenses and not deductible, even if the life insurance is required as collateral for a business loan. It is important to add this to the total cost of borrowing. If the doctor can't get more life insurance and the existing life insurance is needed to protect the family, then giving the lender first dibs on that death benefit will put the family at risk. Similarly with disability insurance, it's very difficult for some doctors to acquire it, and it is expensive. So if the lender is demanding that disability insurance be assigned or purchased to cover the potential loss of payments, it makes the loan significantly more expensive, although it would not seem so based on the interest rates alone.

Many times, business loans are set up with a balloon requirement for full repayment in five or ten years or to refinance the loan at whatever the future interest rates are. But there's nothing to prevent rates from rising. It's difficult to control expenses in your business if your borrowing costs are changing for the worse.

Sometimes a bank will offer a doctor a loan, and as part of the terms there will be strings attached that will state, in effect, "You have to open a business checking account with our bank or you have to do all of the practice's credit card processing with us." The terms of the loan may be very attractive, but some of the other services offered by the bank may not be as competitive. Credit card processing during a 20-year loan may end up costing you significantly more than the difference in interest rates from a more independent lender.

Those are just a few things that doctors may not be aware of when they are shopping for a business loan. A loan is often presented to the doctor as "take it or leave it" or "this is the industry standard and everybody does it this way, and all our competitors have the same sorts of things in their loan agreements." Sometimes that's true; many times it's not true.

Doctors who decide they need to do these things to stay in business or grow their business should at least understand clearly what it means to assign life insurance over to the banker. And understand that a requirement to buy additional insurance is an expense that will not really be disclosed on the estimate from the bank. I often see the choice of lender come down to a quarter-percent of interest rate, and so much more should be involved in an intelligent decision.

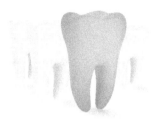

CHAPTER 7

CASH FLOW AND INVESTMENTS

Everyone understands that it takes money to run a financial plan, but where will it come from? With so many competing demands on time and money, it can often feel impossible to find the right balance.

It is essential to take action *immediately* and to start funding one's future. This chapter will reveal how an investor can find significant money right away to fund a financial plan. I'm talking about saving year in and year out to successfully fund a plan over a 20-year career, not just a couple thousand dollars here and there.

Once the dental practice is making money, the doctor basically has three choices for what to do with the profit: (1) spend it: on something like a car or a child's education; (2) invest it: in a retirement fund or brokerage account; or (3) put it back into the practice.

From a planning perspective, it's important to improve the dental practice so that it cannot only generate enough to provide for the doctor's lifestyle but also provide sufficient cash flow to invest outside of the dental practice in a sheltered account, where it can grow into the amount needed for retirement.

IMPROVING THE CASH FLOW

Doctors are very practical and want a framework for deciding which opportunities to choose to improve their business and cash flow. It can be as simple as this:

First, if you are spending money on the practice, it's either (1) a business investment or (2) a business expense. It's an investment if it either (1) grows the practice, helping to generate more collections or (2) improves the standard of care for patients. If the outlay does neither of those, it's probably a business expense.

A business investment might be a marketing campaign that brings in new patients, a street sign that attracts new patients, the learning of new procedures to pursue highly profitable dentistry, and safety equipment or digital radiography that improves the standard of care. Those are clearly investments in the practice.

Things that are not necessarily an investment in the practice—although sometimes they are construed that way—might be remodeling the office, providing employee benefits or new uniforms for the staff, or a new computer system. Another expense that sometimes masquerades as an investment is purchasing the dental office where the doctor practices. I say masquerades, because ownership seems like a good idea, but the building does not grow the practice. Office ownership generally does not generate new income. Your patients don't directly benefit because you own the building.

A second key concept that doctors must understand is the difference between a fixed and a variable cost. A fixed cost, such as rent, is the same no matter how many patients you see, if any. The rent must be paid. A business loan must be paid. Many times, staff costs are fixed. The practice must pay wages, health care, and other benefits of the staff regardless of how productive they are. Variable costs include lab fees and consumable supplies. The more you produce, the higher the variable expense. Having a good grasp of the fixed and variable costs involved in running your dental office can help you improve profitability.

Average cost and marginal cost is also an important distinction. Many dentists are trying to achieve an overhead benchmark of 60 percent on the average, meaning an average profit of 40 percent. So if a million dollars is coming in, $600,000 goes to overhead and staff costs, and $400,000 is left to compensate the doctor or reinvest in the dental practice. That 60 percent overhead is the average cost. Marginal cost is the expense of doing one more procedure—how much it costs to treat one more patient. Because of operational inefficiencies or slack in the schedule, marginal costs are almost always purely variable. To see more patients, the doctor does not need to schedule additional staff time or buy more equipment. The rent doesn't go up. The marginal cost generally is just the lab bill and the consumables bill, which might total 15 percent. So average costs are 60 percent. The marginal cost is only 15 percent.

Third, I will go into detail on practice valuation in chapter 12, but for now take note of this central truth: All things being equal, a practice that collects more money is worth more money. The value of the practice is strongly correlated to its recent history of annual collections. A practice that is collecting a million dollars a year is worth significantly more than a practice that is collecting $600,000. There are a number of valuation techniques to consider, but in general, doctors must understand that their practice is worth what their practice does.

With these key principles in mind, let's look at strategies for improving cash flow and finding the money that the doctor needs to run a financial plan.

One thing that we should talk about is the impact of improving the efficiency of the dental office by reducing overhead. Many doctors will look at how much they are paying for supplies. A doctor spending at the national average might be paying 6 percent of revenues for supplies to practice dentistry.

If they are at anything above 6 percent for supplies, many doctors will fixate on lowering the ratio. They will try to save 10 percent on supplies, negotiating with vendors and searching for Internet deals. The problem is that when you are saving 10 percent of 6 percent, only about one half of one percent or less will go to the bottom line. Sometimes thriftiness does make a difference; particularly if the amount that the doctor is spending on supplies is significantly over 6 percent. That's a red flag that should be analyzed and corrected, but cutting costs alone will not generate enough money for the doctor to run a successful financial plan. It's a half a percent, and half a percent is not enough to make a difference.

Another operational place to look to improve business cash flow is reducing the accounts receivable, or AR. This is the uncollected money that is owed to the practice. That's money that could be reinvested or put to good use. The longer it remains uncollected, the less likely it is to be collected. According to Linda Miles, if there's more than two weeks of production in accounts receivable, that's probably too much. Reducing that figure will improve the cash flow and free up money to do other things.

As we examined in the previous chapter, restructuring debts can also improve cash flow. Many doctors only focus on repaying business loans. If they pay the loan off in five years, they will get a significantly lower interest rate than if they pay the loan off in 10 or 15 years. The problem is, the cash payment every month to pay back the loan in five years is significantly higher. Many times, just restructuring business debt can free up money to fully fund a financial plan.

Improving the tax treatment of the money that moves through the business can make a significant impact on doctors' lifestyles, how quickly they gain wealth, and whether they can hold on to it. I'll discuss the relevance of tax planning in detail in chapter 10.

Better operations can also have a significant impact on cash flow. I have a master's degree in operations research, which has taught me the importance of focusing first on changes that make the biggest difference in outcome. The single best place to focus in the quest for better profits is to improve the operations of the dental office.

START BY LOOKING AT MARKETING, SCHEDULING, CASE ACCEPTANCE, AND THE RULE OF THREE

Although it is important to begin now, it is also important to understand that a sustainable increase in cash flow may take a long while to achieve. In an interview I conducted with Scott J. Manning, MBA of Franklin, TN, he suggests that it may take up to five years of focused effort to achieve the lifestyle practice that you need. Scott believes that cash flow can be increased by marketing to those patients who value good oral health and high-quality dentistry. Once you've gotten better patients, it's important to keep them coming back by having a practice that is patient centered. Scott believes that a patient-centered practice will produce more per hour than one that is clinically centered. His approach is to work on developing a continuous stream of referrals from patients' family members, friends, and coworkers as well as referrals from staff members and other health-care partnerships.

As advocated by my friend and dental practice management expert, Linda Miles, with whom I launched the Dental Business Network in 2006, scheduling makes the most of each hour. Strive to eliminate open chair time with the pending appointment system in your software. Fill openings in the hygiene and doctor's schedule within minutes of a change in the schedule. Don't move already scheduled patients in the following days/weeks to fill openings. Use the nonscheduled patients in the pending system. Otherwise, you teach scheduled patients to move their own appointment, which perpetuates even more open chair time. Utilize your well-trained dental assistants to their limit as defined by your state's dental practice act. Training and delegation are the keys to more productive scheduling and better use of the doctor's time. Gaps in the schedule reduce productivity. There are only so many hours of staff time and only so many clinical hours that the doctor can provide. By better scheduling that time, the office will get more profit per hour.

Go to clinical CE courses to hone your skills and increase your speed. "You don't have to be slow to be good." Efficiency and attention to detail actually improve when speed increases. You may find it makes sense to add staff. It's an expense that will boost your own productivity and greatly improve marginal hourly productivity.

Another way of increasing the productivity per hour, suggested to me by dental consultant Darren Kaberna of Accelerate My Practice, is to schedule quadrant dentistry versus single tooth dentistry. Quadrant dentistry, or doing more than one tooth at a time, is more profitable per hour than treating a single tooth each visit. It also boosts the doctor's productivity substantially.

Kaberna says he often will go into a dental office and look at the records of what has been recommended and what the patient accepted. He finds that case acceptance might average 40 percent. That means patients agree to 40 percent of the treatment that a doctor recommends but do not go ahead with 60 percent of it. Kaberna's method of training the staff helps some practices to improve that case acceptance rate to 50 percent, which translates into a 25 percent increase in profit. By just focusing on the most beneficial changes, the doctor will be able to do more highly productive dentistry and generate more revenue.

In an interview with Jonathan Vanhorn, a CPA in Little Rock, Arkansas, he suggests using the "Rule of Three" in the hygiene department. He says the rule of three works like this:

- Rule of Three #1—A well-running hygiene department should be producing around one-third of the total production for most dental practices, the exception being specialty and niche practices.

- Rule of Three #2—Ideally, each hygienist on the team should be compensated about one-third of the revenue that they are generating (including benefits and payroll taxes).

- Rule of Three #3—No hygienist should have more than three open hours a week when booking out appointments (including cancellations and broken appointments). Vanhorn focuses on getting the hygiene department's collections and compensation into congruence with the rest of the practice for best profitability.

The practice also needs to look at upgrading fees and the procedures regularly. If a doctor raises a fee by 5 percent, most of that money will go straight to the bottom line and not be consumed by overhead. To maintain profitability, therefore, it is important that the doctor update the amount received per procedure, per hour.

Another way to improve cash flow is to institute a group practice model. With more than one doctor working in the same office, the average fixed cost of the office tends to go down. The office can extend the hours and have multiple staffs, without the need to buy more equipment. There is generally less overhead cost in a group practice, which means more profit for the owners.

It's a model advocated by a lot of dental practice management consultants. A problem with the group practice business model is that most doctors just are not wired that way. Many aren't comfortable in a group with other dentists. Many are content being the sole leader of the dental practice.

IS A MANAGEMENT CONSULTANT A GOOD INVESTMENT?

I know a lot of dental practice management consultants. They might charge as much as $50,000 to work with a practice for a year to fix some of the productivity issues, improving cash flow, efficiency, scheduling, or office harmony. Is the consulting fee a good investment?

Let's say that the consultant hopes to improve collections by at least $200,000. How much does the dental practice profit? The average profit of 40 percent on that amount, as I explained earlier, would be $80,000. After paying the $50,000 fee, the practice would be $30,000 ahead after the year. A $30,000 improvement doesn't seem like it would be worth the pain involved to make meaningful change within the practice. Fortunately, the math doesn't work that way. The office is not adding staff or buying more technology; it is just spending more on consumables and supplies. We need to be talking about the marginal profit of 85 percent, which would be $170,000. And so, after paying the consultant $50,000, the profit is $120,000 for the year. Additionally, the practice probably can sustain this level of collections year in and year out if it continues to follow the consultant's advice, so in the ensuing years, the reoccurring annual profit would be the full $170,000.

That's the kind of money that the doctor needs to improve the practice and run a financial plan. There's no way to grow a dental practice without investing some money and improving operations. Anything that can grow the practice should be considered as an investment, and the doctor should look at fixed and variable costs as a way of determining whether that investment will make a difference.

WHERE TO PUT THE MONEY

Now let's say the practice is making $170,000 more than it was. The doctor has three choices: pay taxes on it and spend it, reinvest it into the business, or invest it outside the practice.

If the practice can generate more profit, it could make sense to invest more of that profit back into the business to further improve cash flow or the standard of care. Sometimes the smartest thing a doctor can do is to push all of the profit back into the business, because in just a few years, collections will be significantly higher.

It's clear that a doctor must start saving early if the goal is to go from zero to, say, $4 million by setting aside income. For at least the first decade of his or her career, the growth of the account will be driven more by the savings rate than by what the investments are doing inside it. In other words, if the doctor is saving $30,000 each year, whether that account goes up or down by 10 percent is of minor consequence when the following year another $30,000 of new investment comes in. This is because, emotionally, investors won't panic as long as their statements show a nominal increase year-over-year. Until the investor's account totals at least $300,000, a 10 percent drop in the market will not cause the year-over-year balance to drop.

The most important thing is getting the money into a spot where it can grow—just stick with an efficient combination of low-cost, diversified investments. Doctors should have a diversified mix of investments inside of their accounts, chosen with the advice of a financial consultant, though it should be noted that diversification does not guarantee a profit or protect against a loss. Doctors should focus on what they do best, which is making the money through dentistry. Just as dentistry is a specialty, so are portfolio management, mathematical modeling, and investor counseling. It takes years to develop expertise and wisdom in either field. Many do-it-yourself investors do significantly worse after fees and taxes than those who delegate asset allocation and investment management to a competent financial advisor.

If the market is going up, people tend to buy whatever is going up. If stocks are going up, the new money goes into stocks. If real estate is going up, the new money goes into real estate. There is always some next big thing, but it takes diversification to control downside risk. In a recession, investors may be tempted to sell at the bottom because they can't take it anymore—and then they miss the recovery.

After 2008, it took about four years for the people who stuck to a diversified portfolio to get their money back, and that was a severe downturn. Investors know they should buy low and sell high. It's hard to follow this strategy and avoid the "sell low buy high" traps without the ongoing help, support, and wisdom of a trusted financial advisor. Without good counsel, it's easy to make the same mistakes as everybody else.

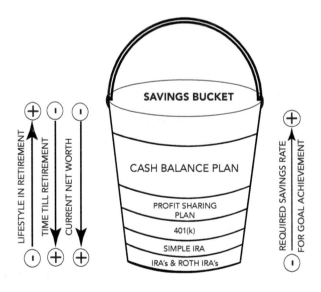

In general, here are some investment tools that I like:

- Qualified retirement plans allow your savings to grow free of taxes until the money is withdrawn. It's easy to set up a SIMPLE IRA. However, the amount you can save each year will not be enough for you to retire. So maybe the first couple of years that you are in practice, having a SIMPLE IRA makes a lot of sense. But after that, you either will not be saving enough, or you will be saving on an after-tax basis when you could be saving on a pre-tax basis. A 401(k) plan is common in a dental office. And basically, the doctor is able to put money away on a pre-tax basis. In 2015, it's $18,000 for those under 50 and an additional $6,000 per year for people over 50. In addition, the practice will give every employee a match. And so it's a very good way of accumulating money needed for retirement. And the money, once it's in the account, grows without tax.

- Profit-sharing plans work well after the doctor has maxed out the 401(k) deferral. In general, doctors can get about another $30,000 into a profit-sharing plan pre-tax. A negative is that they have to share some of the profits with the staff. With a 401(k), you don't need to pay a match unless the employee is contributing, which many on the staff do not do. But with a profit-sharing plan, you must share with eligible employees regardless of their payroll deferral.

- A Roth 401(k) is a good idea for doctors who are able to put away even more than the approximate $53,000 they can save through a combination of 401(k) and profit sharing. You contribute to a Roth with after-tax money, and after the 5-year minimum holding period a 59 ½ year old can usually withdraw it free of income tax.

- A cash balance pension plan is another option for highly productive doctors. This is an additional retirement plan that the doctor can set up in his office and can save significantly more money on a pre-tax basis, between $50,000 and $150,000 per year for the doctor's benefit. When you are trying to save money, it is significantly easier to save money on a pre-tax basis than on an after-tax basis. That is why I like defined benefit pension plans for dental offices.

- Tax-sheltered tools such as 529 plans for college savings are a great way of putting money aside. The money grows without tax for qualified educational expenses as defined by the IRS, but the negative is that you have to use after-tax money to fund these college savings vehicles. After-tax money for most doctors is extremely expensive, because their marginal tax rates are significantly higher.

- The next thing to look at could be an after-tax brokerage account. Remember that you can use these investments without restriction, and you will pay taxes on the growth as you go.

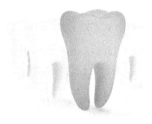

CHAPTER 8

TO BUY OR TO RENT?

N ow that a dentist owns his or her practice, it might seem like a good idea to purchase the building where the dental office is located. Sometimes it is a good idea—but frequently, it is quite the opposite.

It is important to understand how the ownership of a dental office, whether a standalone building or an office condo in a strip mall, will impact the doctor's ultimate retirement or sale of his dental practice in transition. Ideally, the ownership of the dental office should enhance and diversify the business plan of the practice and the doctor's personal financial plan. It should make it better, not restrict what the doctor can do.

RISKY EXPECTATIONS

I know a dentist who bought a practice and was renting the building from the doctor who sold the practice. It turned out, however, that the building had problems that the owner was unwilling to remedy, and so the younger dentist left, taking the business, equipment, and patients to a new location. The dentist who sold the practice had felt confident that he would have a tenant forever and would be able to live off the rental income in retirement. Instead, he had to find another tenant and will still have to repair the known problem with the building. Such arrangements are inherently risky for retired dentists.

Consider, too, that as a building owner, you could be called upon at any hour of the day to deal with maintenance problems. The role of a landlord is considerably different than the role of an owner-operator. For simplicity's sake, seriously consider selling the building to the dentist who buys the practice.

TAKING A HARD LOOK

There clearly can be benefits to ownership. As equity grows in the building, the doctor has the opportunity to borrow against it to fund the expansion of the practice or modernize it. That can improve cash flow and make the practice more valuable.

Many doctors, however, focus on paying off the mortgage loan as quickly as possible. They could be stunting the growth of cash flow of the business that way. Equity might be thought of as an opportunity to fund expansion, renovation, and new equipment.

Every practice is unique. Some doctors feel selling an interest in the building to an associate doctor who then pays some of the overhead cost may be a good way of binding the associate to the practice and to the practice acquisition. Many associates will feel more committed when they own both a portion of the business and a portion of the building.

But does owning the building improve the quality of patient care? Does it help grow the practice? The answer to both questions, generally, is no. Often the decision isn't based on a cash flow analysis but on the way the doctor feels about renting versus buying. Whether the doctor or a third party owns the building, it doesn't improve patient care. And sometimes it's more expensive to own than to rent. If so, that means there's less cash to reinvest in the business, put into the 401(k) plan, spend on innovative equipment, or invest in new procedures and technologies.

TAX AND LIABILITY CONSIDERATIONS

In the year when the doctor is selling a practice, he or she is also typically earning a lot of money from dentistry because the value of the business is in proportion to recent earnings. To get maximum value for a dental practice, a doctor needs to earn a lot of money in the last year before the sale. If the sale of the building happens in the same tax year as the sale of the practice, the doctor ends up paying potentially higher taxes on that capital gain. It could make far more sense to time the sale of the building for the following year, after retirement, or at another time when the doctor will have less taxable income.

It's a mistake to have the dental practice, generally a corporation, own the dental office. If there were a lawsuit against the corporation, all the assets of the corporation could be lost in that lawsuit. So having a significantly valuable dental office as an asset of the S corporation doesn't generally make sense, due to that risk.

WORDS OF CAUTION

In weighing ownership versus renting, the doctor must take a close look at the return on investment. What would be the difference in cash flow? At retirement, how much money could be generated from the real estate?

There are significant realtor commissions, transaction costs, and tax considerations associated with selling a piece of real estate or renting it out to a third party. It all must be considered before a doctor commits to ownership.

Leasing might be cheaper per month than owning, when you calculate the cost of financing, interest, property taxes, and maintenance associated with owning the office. Leasing also can be more flexible if the doctor decides, at some point in a 30-year career, to change locations. A lease also provides flexibility if the practice outgrows the space or needs less space. As a renter, a doctor sometimes can negotiate upgrades for which the property owner will pay. As the owner, the doctor would pay for those up front and out of pocket.

Commercial real estate is illiquid, and its value is economically sensitive, and often the best time to sell may not be when the doctor wants to do so. The dentist might not be retiring when the real estate market is best. Because an existing lease for a dental office can be transferred to the new practice owner, leasing disconnects the selling doctor from that aspect of the business cycle.

A lot of doctors are comfortable taking on the debt of a commercial mortgage, but often it makes little sense to do so, especially if the doctor is nearing retirement. The loan could complicate the doctor's ability to retire, and if the doctor passes away, the loan will complicate matters for the family. Remember, too, that with that much money tied up in a single building, the doctor hardly has diversification of investments. The illiquid real estate investment is at considerably more risk than if it were spread into other investments. Sometimes, the lower overhead of leasing can free up money for those investments.

If the doctor is going to own the building, it is better to avoid owning it in one's own name and have a separate entity like an LLC hold the property as an asset protection strategy. If you are leasing, of course, you don't have that protection need. And leasing keeps things simple for the valuation of a dental practice. It's quicker and easier for the buyer to understand the deal.

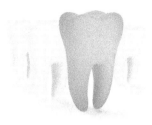

CHAPTER 9

INSURANCE REASSURANCE

Insurance is a protection against the big risks that could wipe out a dentist financially. Doctors don't need to insure their cell phone or computer, but it can make great sense to buy flood, liability, and health insurance.

However, the most important asset for a dentist who has a six-figure income is himself. The way for dentists to protect themselves is generally through long-term disability insurance—and it is best to get as much disability insurance coverage as possible.

Disability insurance is subject to both financial and medical underwriting. Underwriting requires the doctor to be healthy (medical underwriting) with documented income from corrective dentistry (financial underwriting). Additionally, to reduce its risk that a doctor will go on or not come off claim, the insurance company will not insure more than about two-thirds of the doctor's income from dentistry.

Unlike life insurance, where you can often buy as much coverage as you would like, disability insurance is limited. The insurance company wants to make sure the doctor has an incentive to return to work. Most important is the definition of disability in the policy; own-occupation is best. The insurance company might hedge the definition of disability in such a way that it does not have to pay if the doctor can do something else besides corrective dentistry.

Many doctors have the ability to use pre-tax money from their practice to pay their disability insurance premiums as an employee benefit. But if a doctor does that and then goes on claim, the disability benefit will be subject to income taxation. Because the payout is already limited due to financial underwriting, the taxation makes it even more difficult for a doctor on claim to sustain a standard of living. Most doctors pay disability insurance premiums with after-tax money.

LIFE INSURANCE

Life insurance, quite simply, protects loved ones against the loss of income if the insured were to die, and it is a valuable estate planning tool to provide liquidity of assets to cover taxes and other needs. There are two fundamental types of life insurance: term and permanent. Term insurance can have an option to convert to permanent.

Term insurance policies

With term insurance, the named beneficiaries get the death benefit if the policyholder dies within the term of coverage. If a family is dependent on the doctor's income from dentistry, it might be a good idea to get term insurance. The cost of the premium depends on the insured's age and health history, the amount of insurance purchased, and the length of the term.

A financial advisor can calculate how much insurance is needed. Generally, most doctors who have business debt and a family are likely to have a calculated need of $2 million to $5 million worth of coverage, depending on age, size of the family, standard of living, and business and personal debts. Most of that coverage initially should probably be in term insurance, which is cheaper than permanent insurance, but it may make sense to have some of both.

In general, I see policies of more than $2 million for doctors in their 30s, 40s, and early 50s. Once they become wealthier, they are in a position where they can self-insure and won't need as much death benefit.

Permanent insurance policies

Permanent life insurance pays a death benefit when the doctor dies and is not restricted to a term. There are three variables to a permanent life insurance policy: (1) the premium, generally paid with after-tax money; (2) the death benefit, which is generally protected from income taxes but not necessarily from estate taxes; and (3) the cash value, which the policy accumulates over time.

Those three variables are interrelated. Doctors who pay a high premium generally will get, over time, a higher death benefit or higher cash value or both. So if they are putting $1,000 per month into a life insurance policy that has an insurance cost of around $100 a month comparable to a term life policy, they will accumulate cash value over time.

On the other hand, if the policy owner paid a lower premium (and a lot of insurance policies let the premium vary from month to month), they will get a smaller cash value accumulation over time. Therefore, a lower premium does not necessarily mean the life insurance is better.

The minimum premium can go down if there is significant cash value inside the policy. You have much more flexibility with regard to what the monthly premiums could be. You could even suspend the premiums and still maintain the coverage for a time. If you have a significant cash value inside of a life insurance policy, you can withdraw, on a tax-advantaged basis, some of that money for other purposes.

For example, for a given policy year, if the death benefit is held constant, the required premium will decrease as the cash value increases. The premiums for life insurance are almost always after-tax expenses. If there's cash value inside of the insurance policy, it can grow income tax-deferred.

Permanent life insurance can make sense for those doctors who are in a group practice as a way of funding buy–sell agreements. An associate may need permanent life insurance if you will need some way of buying out your partner in the future.

Also, it can be beneficial to use the cash value of permanent insurance as an investment because any potential cash value growth is tax deferred. As more cash value accumulates in the policy, the difference between the promised death benefit and the accumulated cash inside the policy gets smaller. This means that the insurance company has less money at risk, and the minimum required premium gets smaller.

In general, if the internal costs of the policy are less than the expenses and taxes for a brokerage account investment outside of an insurance policy, using life insurance as an accumulation vehicle can make sense. Generally, having more cash value inside of a permanent life insurance policy gives you better performance with the variables inside the insurance policy, and it gives the policy owner greater flexibility.

Converting a policy

Most of my clients have term life insurance. Sometimes because of a client's individual circumstances it can make sense to have permanent life insurance as well. A term policy can, many times, be converted in full or in part into a permanent policy. A million-dollar, 20-year term policy, for example, can be converted by keeping half as term and converting the other half to permanent. Conversion could be a good option if the doctor decides later that he or she needs permanent life insurance or that the benefits of having permanent life insurance make sense for their particular situation.

Doctors who are less healthy for their age than when they obtained the term insurance may find that converting a term policy to a permanent one is a better option than going through separate underwriting for a new policy.

Conversion can also be a means of maintaining insurance after marrying or having children late in life. Because our health history changes over time it can be hard to get underwritten for affordable life insurance as we age, so this alternative strategy may be needed. If the doctor has some existing insurance through a group policy or an old term policy, that policy can sometimes be kept alive through conversion. Doctors who are working and have some group insurance may be able to take it with them when they leave their employer.

Beneficiaries

The beneficiaries on the insurance policy are very important. Beneficiary designation generally bypasses whatever estate plan the doctor has set up. Those listed on the beneficiary designation form with the insurance company will get the policy benefit at the insured's death. If the beneficiaries are out of date, the doctor runs the risk of disinheriting the spouse and children.

So it's important to make sure that those intended beneficiary designations are current. I have often found that those designations are not correct and consistent with what the client wants. When the policy was set up, the agent who took the policy needed a name for the beneficiaries, and those were never changed. Many times, the client will assume that the attorney will change the investment account and insurance beneficiary designations. Generally, it is not part of their responsibility to change the beneficiary forms on all of the clients. And sometimes the life insurance doesn't end up going through clients' estate plan because of a gap in who was responsible for making changes.

OTHER PROTECTIONS

Another type of insurance is liability coverage—business liability, malpractice insurance, and personal liability. If the doctor or business were to get sued, the insurance company would be first in line to provide payment, and the doctor's assets would be next.

If the doctor has significant hard assets, like real estate, it is important to have proper property and casualty coverage and flood insurance. Sometimes the doctor will work hard to get the house paid off and then won't insure it properly.

Long-term care insurance is important for a lot of doctors. My opinion, as a planner, is that this type of insurance should only be considered once life insurance and disability insurance needs are addressed. It's more important to have life insurance and disability insurance in place. But at a certain point, it's really important to anticipate the need, the contingency of a long-term or extended health-care event, and the benefit of long-term care insurance. For most clients, I want to have a solid strategy in place by the time they are 50 years old for addressing extended health-care events or a long-term-care need. Anyone younger than that should be focused on saving enough money for long-term goals and putting other types of insurance in place.

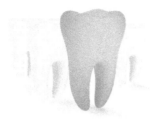

CHAPTER 10

TAX PLANNING

Note: I am not a tax professional. This chapter contains educational ideas to consider along with your team of tax professionals based on your situation.

If you are not proactively doing formal tax planning, you are almost certainly paying too much in taxes. The default action in the absence of tax planning tends to primarily benefit the government.

You may not be taking advantage of all of the available tax deductions or maintaining your records correctly, which could trigger a costly audit. Tax planning helps to keep the profit and cash in your own hands, so you can improve patient care, reinvest in your business, and better pursue your personal financial goals.

If a doctor is earning money but having trouble saving it, the solution—other than improving the top line growth of the dental practice—is to look at tax-planning and tax-reduction strategies. Even if the doctor can only find $5,000 more a year in deductions, that can make a significant difference year in and year out in the cash flow from the business. Saving money over decades can make all the difference.

A SPECIAL RELATIONSHIP WITH THE IRS

In general, the IRS taxes profits. Anything that's collected, minus properly documented business expenses that the IRS allows, is profit that is subject to taxation at various levels. However, the IRS favors business owners with more options than it gives associate dentists who are employees. The rules change every year, but many expenses are eligible for a business deduction. There are plenty of legitimate tax-reduction strategies that can be helpful to the self-employed dental practitioner.

Generally, business owners are more likely to be audited by the IRS than are comparably earning associates who get a paycheck in someone else's dental practice. Business owners need to understand that because they are subject to an IRS audit, they must have perfect records all the time in a format that the IRS might want to see. Tax records must be kept up to date throughout the year—not just in April. The doctor should not try to reconstruct things after being called for an audit. It is almost impossible to reconstruct something done several years ago to meet the IRS documentation requirements. Doctors must adopt the habit of doing the paperwork as they go. It's too hard to try to catch up or do it once a year.

From time to time, dentists do get audited by the IRS, and in general, an audit means lost time from the practice because the doctor must focus on meeting the requirements of the IRS. Audits are stressful. Knowing and following the rules is work, but that work is less stressful than being surprised that the delegated paperwork did not get done correctly.

If a doctor is audited, it does not necessarily mean that he will pay more taxes than he otherwise would. The IRS may just be checking for verification, and if the documentation is in order, there is no reason to expect an additional tax bill.

The best strategy is to comply with all the rules all the time and get all the tax deductions possible. It is time well spent to learn more about these rules and some of the strategies that a business owner can systematize and easily follow.

TAXES TO CONSIDER

The doctor, of course, must understand the nature of federal, state, and local taxes. Generally, federal tax rates are progressive. In other words, if you don't have a lot of taxable income, you won't be in a top tax bracket. But if you do have significant taxable income, your marginal tax may become more and more onerous. You can move from 25 to 28 percent to 33 to 39.6 percent in marginal tax rates.

Another important tax to understand is capital gains tax, which occurs when a capital asset is sold for more than its tax basis. These taxes occur when the doctor sells an asset for more than he paid for it or for more than his adjusted basis. Generally capital gains taxes are paid on the difference between the adjusted sale price and the cost basis.

The doctor also may be dealing with recapture taxes. This is a tax on the sale of something for more than its depreciated value. In other words, if the doctor buys something for $1,000, depreciates it to $0 for a business purpose, and then sells it in his business for $500, then he must pay recapture taxes on the $500 that he previously depreciated to the IRS.

Other taxes that the doctor must consider include the sales taxes on the purchase of new items, payroll taxes, new taxes for the Affordable Care Act, and property taxes on real estate and office equipment.

UNDERSTANDING TAX ENVIRONMENTS

Tax planning involves making better choices about what to do in various tax environments. Each environment has different rules, advantages, and disadvantages. Moving money from one environment to another can cost more if you don't understand these rules.

The first is the **personal environment**. You buy a car or take a vacation with after-tax money in your personal checking account.

Another tax environment is the **tax-deferred environment**. These are things like qualified plans, 401(k) plans, and IRAs. These are subject to tax once the asset is pulled out of that environment.

Another is the **tax-free environment**, and these are things like Roth IRA's, Roth 401(k)s, 529 plans for college, and some inherited assets, and sometimes municipal bonds are also in a tax-free environment.

A fourth tax environment is the **corporate or business tax environment**, an important one for doctors operating a dental practice. You should work very closely with the CPA and bookkeeper to make sure that all the rules are followed and that no additional taxes or unnecessary taxes are generated by operating this business.

The fifth tax environment is a catchall that you could call the **tax-favored environment**. These are things like long-term capital gains taxes, taxes on passive income from rental real estate, the accelerated depreciation of business assets, the taxation of interest on debts, and the tax-favored nature of annuities or permanent life insurance.

BASIC STRATEGIES

Most of the basic strategies involve a couple of principles. One is that under the US tax structure, the more income you have in a given tax year, the higher your marginal tax rate.

This is different from the effective tax rate. The effective tax rate—that is the average of how much money one pays per dollar of total income—is usually significantly less. The effective tax rate might only be about 17 percent, whereas the marginal tax rate might be 25 percent. For example, with the effective tax rate on $100,000 of taxable income, the total tax due is nearly $17,000, not $25,000.

A basic strategy is to structure business expenses to make the most of tax deductions. Business expenses are tax deductible against the revenues of the business. If you have a choice, it's almost always more powerful to take a deduction as a business deduction rather than as a personal deduction. That is mainly because business deductions can reduce payroll taxes and self-employment taxes. Personal deductions are usually subject to phase-outs and other rules, and they always come after payroll taxes are paid.

A second strategy that's common for CPAs to use is income shifting—moving taxable income from an entity or person that has a high tax rate to an entity or person with a lower marginal tax rate.

Some doctors might shift earned income to their children and get a business tax deduction at the doctor's tax rate, while the child pays the tax at a lower rate. By doing that, the doctor can provide earned income for minor children (money that the doctor would have otherwise spent or given to them), which can be used for their college education or their retirement savings.

The third basic tax strategy is tax deferral. With tax deferral, investments are able to grow without cost of current taxation. For example, if an investment has an expected return of 8 percent but is subject to 25 percent taxation, the after-tax effective long-run total return on that investment would be closer to 6 percent.

A classic example of this is a 401(k) contribution. New money is added to the qualified plan, and the tax deductions are realized at the doctor's top marginal tax rate. Then the money is allowed to grow inside the 401(k) plan until retirement, so it increases without tax at a higher rate than it would if it were in the taxable or personal environment. And when the money is needed in retirement, generally the doctor will have a significantly lower effective tax rate, even if the marginal tax rates are the same or higher and will pay less tax on that money.

The fourth basic strategy is the timing of taxable events. For example, it may make sense to take a deduction in a year when the doctor has really high taxable income to help offset the income. By timing such taxable events, the doctor can even out the tax burden from year to year.

Another basic strategy is simply business entity selection. Doctors have a choice of how their businesses, their dental practices, will be taxed. Generally, the practice chooses to be taxed as a S-corporation. Other than profits being passed through to the corporation owner, the potential benefit of this business form is the reduction in payroll taxes. Sometimes doctors choose a C-corporation and, in general, the potential benefit of that is that doctors can have higher-level business deductions for employee benefits program. Or they might decide to be taxed as a sole proprietor, which sometimes provides better income shifting strategies, especially if the owner's minor children work in the practice.

The point of all these tax strategies is to free up cash flow to increase the savings rate toward your investments. Repeated year in and year out, this tends to be a great financial planning strategy.

DON'T WAIT FOR THE PAIN

Unfortunately, I have found that many CPA firms neglect the importance of tax planning. They prepare the forms and sometimes do bookkeeping, but rarely will they do formal tax planning for the doctor and his business. But tax planning is like hygiene. It is not income tax preparation. Income tax preparation is more like corrective dentistry. If you only see your CPA in April, then your visits are likely to be painful and expensive. If accountants were dentists, you would probably look upon many of them in much the same way as you do those doctors who only perform "drill and fill" dentistry.

It's really important that doctors proactively meet with their accountants to try to develop strategies annually to take advantage of the tax rule changes and opportunities to minimize, shift, and defer taxes or to time taxable events to save money.

I have developed a list of good questions to ask the CPA during a tax-planning conversation:

- How might I benefit from the establishment of an "administrative home office" as my principal place of business?

- How could I increase the fraction of my deductible business auto expenses?

- Am I correctly keeping my personal expenses separate from my corporate expenses? Is my practice reimbursing me correctly?

- What are the tax rules for business travel?

- Could you give me a written professional opinion as to which business entity form would be best for my current situation?

- Is health insurance and long-term-care insurance for family members deductible as a business expense?

- Does a "cost segregation analysis" make sense for my build out or building purchase? Would accelerating the depreciation of assets within my dental office be helpful?

- Am I ready for an IRS audit today? What are my business tax recording requirements, and what do you need from me?

- How might a tax-qualified retirement plan benefit me?

- If I am subject to the Alternative Minimum Tax, how might increasing my business deductions help?

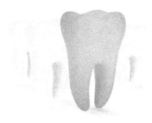

CHAPTER 11

ESTATE PLANNING AND ASSET PROTECTION

Note: I am not a lawyer. This chapter contains educational ideas to consider along with your team of legal professionals based on your situation.

In its most basic form, estate planning is about taking care of the people you love. "Estate planning" is a broad term, which usually encompasses several highly personal legal documents. These legal strategies include asset protection against future creditors, limited liability companies, and other corporate documents; disability and incapacity planning; asset transfer upon death; tax-leveraged gifting strategy; restrictions on those transferred assets to protect beneficiaries; and sometimes special-needs planning.

It's important that everybody understand that they have an estate plan regardless of whether they have prepared one. That's because every state has its own intestate protocol for people who don't have a will. The way I would tell my clients who live in Virginia is, "You can be sure that the state of Virginia has an estate plan for you, but you may or may not like it."

Estate planning will require the assistance of a qualified and smart attorney, especially when it involves how to deal with transferring the dental practice if the doctor were to die suddenly. You cannot properly protect and care for the people you love by doing estate planning on your own. Most doctors who go in to see an attorney really have no idea how the system works. They trust that the estate-planning attorney will know all the relevant facts and discover what is most important to them and develop documents that are both flexible and take advantage of current law.

In general, all assets break down into one or two categories. Some assets are probate property and transfer via a court process when somebody dies. Non-probate property does not move through the court and transfers by other means. Generally, what most people want is for all of their assets to move privately, quickly, and efficiently to the people that they care about without probate.

THE POWER OF TRUSTS

A trust is a legal document set up by the doctor, who is generally the grantor of the trust. A trust provides the doctor with the flexibility of transferring assets in a way that meets the doctor's objectives and can change as the circumstances change.

Assets that are held within a trust are private, as opposed to a will, in which assets become part of the public record in probate court for anyone to examine on the Internet. That publicity includes all of the dentist's assets, all accounts, the addresses of all property, and all of the dentist's debts. A trust provides a way of keeping family matters private from prying eyes.

Another advantage of trusts is they have a built-in succession of trustees, so if one trustee is not available to execute the conditions of the trust, a successor can be found in an orderly way without the use of the courts.

Trusts also can include rules that guide the trustee to distribute the assets in a way that the deceased would want. These rules can protect the estate and the heirs.

Trusts can be revocable or nonrevocable. In a revocable living trust, which is most common, the doctor can change any of the terms, beneficiaries, or assets without going to court. A nonrevocable trust, once it is set up and funded, cannot be changed.

In order to avoid probate and to take advantage of the rules and privacy protections, the trust must be funded, which means that the doctors assets must be either titled in the name of that trust, or the trust can be funded at death via a beneficiary designation form.

Generally, that's one of the biggest problems I see—doctors will have a very elaborate estate plan that's set up by an attorney. They have paid several thousand dollars to a competent law firm for estate plan documents, but because the trust is not funded, the documents would not actually transfer and protect assets for the doctor's heirs. Without asset transfer to the trust, the interests of the heirs cannot be protected. For example, property such as the doctor's residence or vacation home that is in the doctor's name would not go through the trust. Instead, it would transfer via a probate court process.

Almost always, the dental practice shares or membership interest are held as own-name property. For example, if the doctor owns his dental office, it might be owned by an LLC—but the doctor owns the LLC interest personally. That means when the doctor passes away, business ownership will transfer via the probate system.

The other type of property that typically doesn't move through a trust is beneficiary property, such as brokerage accounts, 529 college accounts, 401(k) plans, or IRAs. Those accounts must be owned by an individual, and normally the primary beneficiary is a person. That means that even though the doctor may have an estate plan, whoever is listed as the beneficiary with the investment company is who will get unrestricted access to the money. It doesn't matter what the doctor's will or trust says. Beneficiary property does not protect your heirs from their future creditors, their financial mismanagement, or their future ex-spouses.

When you add up the biggest assets that a doctor has, these are usually a retirement account, the dental office and practice, and the personal residence. And those assets regularly fail to pass through the doctor's estate plan because of failure to take the extra steps of making sure that everything works.

In Virginia, a doctor must own the dental practice. It can't be held in the name of a trust. Usually, if the doctor passes away while owning the dental practice, then the practice must move through probate. One way to avoid that is to have the attorney draft a "transfer on death" document for the doctor's business. It only springs into effect when the doctor passes away and it goes directly to the named beneficiary on the document.

It is a bad situation for a dental practice to go through probate, especially if the doctor wasn't expecting to need to sell it. Usually this is the case when a doctor passes away before retiring and the spouse is left to try to quickly liquidate the practice but lacks the proper authority to do so. Because key staff and patients leave the practice after the owner's death, the value of the dental practice depreciates rapidly. Having to go to a probate court and explain what is being done to operate and transition may destroy a lot of the practice's equity for the surviving family and put a lot of stress on the surviving spouse.

This can be especially problematic if the doctor's will leaves the assets to more people than just the surviving spouse. If some of the property is going to charity and some to adult children or to siblings, then the probate court is likely to order increased scrutiny to protect the interests of all the heirs; this increased court oversight may be expensive and prolonged. The longer a dental practice sits on the market without a buyer, the lower its value will become. This situation can apply even if there's a buy-sell agreement because the person who is compelled to buy the practice will need to purchase that practice from the estate of the survivor. That's why the estate planning documents must be set up in advance.

Another problem is that many revocable living trusts cannot accept and hold S-corporation shares. The trust must be capable of accepting the benefits of the S-corp tax structure. Otherwise, the practice will go through probate. Or if it is accepted by the trust, the IRS may disagree and dissolve the S-corporation status, which can cause all sorts of tax complications. It's important that a doctor who operates his business as an S-corporation and has a revocable living trust makes sure that it has qualified subchapter S-corporation trust provisions or QSST provisions written into it. These allow the revocable living trust to accept the dental practice so that the dental practice can be privately and quickly sold by the trustee.

WHEN THE DOCTOR IS DISABLED

As part of your estate-planning package, you also need to address the prospect of incapacity or disability. This is done through documents that provide a trusted someone with the authority to step in and operate the dental practice, to make financial and medical decisions, and, if need be, to sell the practice on the doctor's behalf.

If the doctor is disabled and these documents don't exist, then the family of the doctor will need to petition the court to get the authority to do these things. The court will more likely put the family of the doctor who is incapacitated under significant scrutiny if they try to sell the practice. It's best to think about this when you are getting your will and estate plan done.

Another part of the package is a living will or an advance health-care directive. These documents vary by state, but in general they set up a person who can make medical decisions for the person who is incapacitated if that person can no longer make these decisions, generally when he or she is terminally ill. A living will is a personal matter. The doctor doesn't have to get a living will, but it's usually a good idea, and it usually doesn't cost the doctor any additional money because it's part of the law firm's estate-planning package. It's also important to remember that if anything changes, the doctor must update the living will.

ASSET PROTECTION

Another important issue is asset protection. This is protection against future creditors. The various measures that the doctor may choose to take depend greatly on the laws of the state. These laws seem to be changing frequently.

Asset protection does not mean complete safety against lawsuits or creditors, but it does reduce the risk. If the doctor is sued, a creditor could take all of the assets that the doctor controls as payment for the judgment. If a corporation or an LLC is sued, then the creditor may force liquidation of the assets inside the corporation to pay the creditors.

There's a difference between a business being sued and the doctor being sued personally. If the doctor follows the corporate legal formalities and the business is sued, only the business assets are generally at risk. If the doctor is sued, both personal and business assets are at risk.

Every dentist's actual risk and perceived risk is different, but it is important to get the basics right before engaging in more elaborate asset protection strategies. There is a lot that can be done without spending a lot of money on elaborate overseas trusts and the like. There are basic or statutory protections that the doctor needs to do first.

The more protected assets that doctors have, the less likely that the doctor will be sued. Lawsuits are expensive to pursue, and if a creditor feels that he is unlikely to collect a substantial judgment, the creditor is less likely to sue. It is more likely that the case will settle out of court or that the litigant will be satisfied with liability insurance proceeds. Taking these basic steps tends to reduce the chance of lawsuits.

It is important to understand which assets are generally not protected. Assets titled in the doctor's own name are unprotected. That includes automobiles; sometimes the house; property held jointly with the spouse; and any accounts, titles, bank accounts, or brokerage accounts that are titled jointly or community property. And just because the doctor's spouse may own assets does not mean that it couldn't be lost to a lawsuit. An asset isn't necessarily protected from the doctor's creditors if the doctor has paid for it, uses it, or controls it.

Any assets that are fraudulently conveyed or gifted after a creditor event happens are unprotected. If you know you are going to get sued and you give away all of your assets, the court may reclaim those assets under the fraudulent conveyance rules.

Many doctors don't understand that assets that are titled in the name of their revocable living trust are completely unprotected. Doctors don't understand that if they are sued personally, their S-corporation or C-corporation shares could be lost because they are unprotected. Assets such as a membership interest in an LLC are unprotected. Any inherited or beneficial IRA accounts in which the doctor is named as a beneficiary is subject to the claims of a creditor and is not protected like qualified retirement accounts.

INSURANCE AS THE CORNERSTONE

The first thing that doctors should be doing is making sure they have the correct amount of liability insurance. That is the cornerstone of an asset protection plan. It provides some protection against loss. It provides a pool of money that could be paid to a creditor. Generally, insurance companies are quite capable of hiring attorneys to defend the doctor against judgment.

Types of insurance that are important to own include a personal umbrella, business umbrella, and malpractice liability policies. These policies have a lot of fine print, and they never cover excluded items.

Liability insurance never covers personal acts or deliberate acts, including things like sexual harassment, age discrimination, assault, or slander. It's important that doctors understand outside of insurance that some states will actually limit a doctor's professional liability. For example, Virginia has a legal cap of one million dollars for professional liability as of 2015. Generally, a doctor would not need professional liability insurance in excess of the statutory limits.

LEGAL TOOLS

There are statutory protections that exempt some assets by law from creditors. These include things like qualified plans, IRAs, 401(k) accounts, the doctor's personal residence, and sometimes their vacation homes. Things such as college funds are sometimes excluded, and sometimes the cash value inside of an insurance policy or the death benefit of an insurance policy are protected from creditors.

Remember that assets that are owned by the corporation are subject to the claims of corporate creditors. Because it's the practice that is most likely to be sued, it's a good strategy to minimize assets owned by the dental practice. It's best to limit the practice to owning just the dental equipment and the doctor's goodwill. If the doctor owns the building, it's best that it is held as a separate entity and not as part of the dental practice.

Another domestic legal tool is a limited liability company or a family limited partnership, LLC, or FLP. These provide charging order protections. Charging order protection means that if the court orders a judgement against the assets of the limited liability company or the family limited partnership the creditor's ability to collect those business assets may be very limited. Once the charging order is issued, the LLC/FLP may not obligated to make payment to the creditor, but the creditor is obligated to pay the taxes on the judgment.

Another domestic legal tool is the irrevocable trust. Anything that is given to a trust and no longer belongs to the doctor is not subject to the claims of the doctor's creditors. Irrevocable trusts can also be set up with what is known as a spendthrift clause, which means that the trusts cannot be compelled to pay out proceeds of the trust to satisfy the needs of the beneficiaries' creditors.

A negative, of course, of an irrevocable trust is that once that asset is transferred into it, the doctor loses control of that asset forever, but it is great protection for the doctor's heirs as part of their estate plan after the doctor's death.

Unfortunately, many people agree to a loss of statutory protections. In general, if a doctor agrees to give up some of his or her rights by signing a contract, the court will uphold that contract regardless of the general rights they might have if they had not signed it. An example is a personal guarantee on a loan. If the doctor signs a personal guarantee, even if the business fails or can't pay the business loan, the doctor could be on the hook because he has personally guaranteed the loan.

Prenuptial or postnuptial agreements are good examples of agreeing to terms where there's a loss of protection. Another example is the cosigning of loans, such as student loans given to children. As a parent, if you cosign a student loan and the student can't pay the loan back for whatever reason, you as the cosigning parent would be expected to repay the debt.

Sometimes partnership agreements have fine print that talks about several liability. If all of your partners go bankrupt and you are the last one with any money, you could be on the hook for paying all of the debts of the partnership. Many times, doctors, especially doctors who invest in real estate deals, find themselves open to several liabilities with their business partners.

I have also seen doctors assign their insurance, especially life insurance or disability insurance proceeds, to satisfy the creditors. This can be unwise. The intent of that life and disability insurance is to meet the doctor's personal needs and the needs of the family, not the requirements of creditors.

PART THREE

FOR WHAT IT'S WORTH

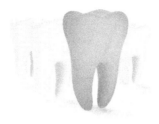

CHAPTER 12

TRANSITIONING YOUR DENTAL PRACTICE

"I haven't decided what I want to do with my dental practice or how much money I'll need or who should buy it or when—so how can I plan my exit? Besides, I don't want to get out now." That's the attitude of many dentists as they contemplate their future and what will become of their practice.

As you near your transition, it is very important that you rethink your financial strategies and reevaluate the financial attitudes that you've used throughout the majority of your career.

Many doctors identify closely with their dental practice. They are ego driven. The practice reflects who they are, and they talk about the practice almost as if it were a person. In my family, the business was the Golden Child. Sometimes, the Golden Child got preference in both attention and resources. Many doctors treat their business like their babies, they sometimes pour money into it, and they spend a lot of discretionary time at the dental office.

But with all of that invested time and money, how much is the business worth, anyway? It's important to find out, even if the doctor doesn't know the particulars of an exit strategy and has no immediate plans for one. Eventually, an exit of some sort is inevitable, and the doctor must get a good idea as to how much money to reinvest back into the practice. Is that new investment to improve patient care or to increase collections and profit or both?

Knowing approximately what the practice is worth helps the doctor to focus on goal achievement, and it also helps the doctor to benchmark the practice and understand how its value and cash flow change over time. The doctor needs to know what the practice is worth throughout his or her career, not just when preparing to sell it.

A doctor should ask this basic question: "What does this dental practice asset do (and not do) for me in reaching my financial goals?" That dispassionate viewpoint will lead to better decisions. First and foremost, the doctor must understand that the sale of the dental practice by itself is seldom going to provide enough money to support retirement. In my experience, the practice might be worth only 10 to 20 percent of the liquid resources that will be needed to maintain the doctor's desired standard of living throughout a 30-year retirement. Most of the doctor's retirement income must come from the sale of other investments, such as mutual funds, and from such sources as a spouse's pension, Social Security benefits, or cash flow from rental real estate.

Throughout the doctor's career, the practice should be used to generate excess cash flow that can be saved or invested outside the practice. From a business and financial planning point of view, that's the best use of the dental practice. By having a dispassionate viewpoint of what the practice is worth, dentists can keep their personal and business lives in better balance.

THE VARIABLES OF VALUATION

It is important to understand how to value the dental practice. There are two schools of thought. One is to get a formal valuation. Most doctors say they don't know what their dental practice is worth because they haven't paid for a formal valuation by a business broker, CPA, or a valuation analyst. Because they don't plan to sell soon, they don't see the need to pay for the formal analysis.

But at some point, a formal valuation does make sense, generally right before retirement or the sale. It's important to understand that a formal valuation is just a professional opinion on what a buyer might be willing to pay at a particular point in time. There are three variables: when, why, and how.

The formal valuation is a snapshot in time. It is really only good for that one date. Valuations tend to have a fairly short shelf life. If the doctor does not act on the formal valuation within a reasonable period, the valuation document will have very little future relevance.

Also, the practice's projected value depends on why the doctor is getting it valued. The value of the business for sale to a third party will be a different number than the value for sale to an associate. It will differ if the valuation is needed for the doctor's divorce. It will differ if it is for a buy-sell agreement between business partners or to settle an estate tax claim with the IRS or to give a portion of the value to a charity. It might be different if the purpose is for an employee stock option program. Even though it is the same business and the same period, you might get several numbers, depending on the purpose of the valuation.

The third variable for a practice valuation is the how. Which valuation method is being used? How sensitive is the result to small variations in the input assumptions? What I've found is that most business brokers or CPAs will use several methods and then take a weighted average to get a specific dollar value.

VALUATION METHODS

There are several formal valuation techniques. One is the market approach, which uses comparable sales. In other words, you can argue that your practice is worth what a similar practice nearby sold for. Another method is the asset approach, or just appraising all the equipment and other hard assets in the dental office. A different approach, important to a dentist's financial plan, might be the income approach. This means that the value of the dental office is based on the owner's discretionary income. The advantage of this approach is that it is much quicker to calculate; formulas are used to determine the value.

Using the discount or capitalization rate is another method. This is much more subjective and depends on the experience of the person doing the valuation. It's important that the doctor understand that even a small change in the capitalization rate or the discount rate can greatly impact the nominal value of the business. A discount rate is a rate of return required to convert future profit into a present value. The capitalization rate is a divisor used to convert a future return into an indication of value. The capitalization rate is supposed to represent the buyer's opportunity cost when considering all the other current investment alternatives.

EVERYTHING IS NEGOTIABLE

When I was the executive officer of a nuclear submarine school in Norfolk, Virginia, I would tell my sailors who wanted to buy a car that there were several factors to consider, including the price, interest rate, down payment, length of the loan, and value of the trade-in. If the sailor focused on the best price or the lowest payment, he might be missing the bigger picture, because the car dealer or the seller can adjust the other variables to compensate.

Similarly, dentists must understand that price is only part of the deal. In the transition of a dental practice, not only is the price negotiable but so are the terms. Whether the doctor structures the sale of the dental practice as an asset sale or a stock sale affects the taxation to the buyer and the seller. Will the seller finance the buyer with an installment loan, or will the buyer have to get bank financing to pay the seller? What sort of business entity will the seller have? What sort of business entity will the buyer have? Will it be an S-corporation, a C-corporation, or a sole proprietorship?

Taxes are one of the biggest factors that impact the amount that the seller will get out of the deal. These include recapture taxes and capital gains taxes and income taxes. Tax rules change all the time. If the seller has an offer and doesn't understand how to negotiate taxable issues, then he almost certainly will end up either getting a lower price or paying the IRS more than necessary.

Another issue involves the owner's discretionary cash flow items and benefits. Will the new owner buy into the practice over time or buy the whole practice in one day and force the seller to walk away from it? Will the selling doctor be signing a covenant not to compete?

Will there be a management contract so that after the senior doctor sells, he will consult for the associate doctor?

Will the transition be active or passive? A passive transition amounts to a letter to patients saying this: "Dr. New Guy is your dentist now. He's good. I sold my practice to him. Please come to the building and get your dental work done." Or will it be an active transition where the selling doctor stays in the practice, talks to each patient, and favorably introduces the buyer? The approach makes a big difference in the success of the transition and the price that the seller should expect. Is any real estate associated with the practice? Is there an office lease? These are some of factors that impact a transition and that are subject to negotiation.

INFORMAL VALUATIONS

A fundamental of any financial plan is a clear understanding of where you are financially at least annually. That way a doctor can measure progress toward personal financial goals. As a CFP® Professional, I track a client's net worth annually; net worth is total assets minus total liabilities. As a business owner, you can't measure your net worth without a current business valuation.

Doctors must understand the value of an informal valuation, one that they don't necessarily have to engage a Chartered Valuation Analyst to get. I provide informal valuations as a part of my financial analysis.

Formula method

To aid business owners in making decisions, I tend to use the historical or the "going regional rate" for the practice to get a snapshot of the practice's value for the doctor's current net worth statement.

In the example below, I might assume that the practice is worth somewhere between 60 percent and 80 percent of the average collections reported on the doctor's most recent corporate tax return. In order to forecast a transition value at the selling doctor's retirement, I assume that the equity that's in the practice will grow at its historical rate of fee growth. For mid-to-late-career doctors, I generally assume that the doctor has a full schedule and that fees will grow at the practice's long-term historical rate.

Example of Formula Valuation for a Mid-Career General Dentist with No Business Debt	
Current collections from tax return	$1,000,000
Assumed historical going rate	70%
Snapshot value ($1M x 70%)	$700,000
Historical rate of fee growth for this dentist with a full schedule	3.63%
Forecasted value of practice in ten years	$1,000,000
Business broker commissions, legal and accounting fees	-10%
Forecast liquidity event subject to federal and state taxes in ten years	**$900,000**

The example above might apply well to many general dentists. Specialist dentists tend to be more referral based or transactional, which means there is less goodwill in the practice. That tends to push their multiple lower, less than 0.6. But their collections are significantly higher than those of a general dentist, so that tends to raise the price of the practice.

It's better to be conservative and assume a lower number. If the doctor's financial plan works when his business is forecast to be worth closer to $600,000 than to $800,000, the plan will certainly work if the doctor ends up getting a million dollars out of the transition.

The net value of the business is important. The doctor's net worth statement must include all of the business debt. If the doctor is going to sell the business through a business broker, then the net amount is the amount collected after repaying business debt and paying the business broker fee.

It's important to understand that business real estate is a separate deal from the operating dental practice and that the building and the rent that the building is generating are based more on the local commercial real estate market than on what the dental practice is doing.

Income method

In informal valuations, the sellers tend to use the formula or going-rate method, however the buyers need to focus on the income valuation methodology.

When I was going to college in the late 1980s, there was a great run-up in real estate values in the Seattle area. People wondered how high real estate prices could get. At the time, people said a Seattle house was worth whatever a Boeing engineer could afford. If an engineer couldn't afford the mortgage payments, it was too expensive. Similarly, the income methodology implies that a dental practice is worth whatever the dentist who operates it makes for a living after paying off all expenses.

It's important that the seller understand that the buyer will probably need to borrow money to pay for the purchase. The seller may decide to lend that money to the borrower, or the borrower might get the cash from the bank. If the buyer's maximum monthly budget for debt service is fixed and the cost of borrowing goes up then the affordable asking price for the dental practice must go down.

Selling doctors need to understand that young doctors have many options and that they can have a good lifestyle and reach financial independence without burden of being business owners. Mathematically speaking, associate employee doctors have the cash flow to achieve financial independence by their late 50s, especially if they begin by fully funding their 401(k) plans right after they get out of school.

The buyer has a financial plan, too, and generally the buyer will need to be compensated what an employee associate dentist would earn in salary. Profits in excess of what the new owner-operator could earn as an associate dentist can be used to service the debt to the selling doctor or to the bank.

A BALANCED APPROACH TO FIXING MONEY MALOCCLUSION

In my experience, I have found that greedy doctors tend to have difficulty in closing the deal with an associate. If the doctor has an idea that the practice is worth a million dollars and drives a really tough bargain, it will be difficult to both find and actually get paid by that buyer. It's important to be reasonable when selling the practice.

Doctors who hang on to their practice past age 70 tend to die in their practice. Without a viable and executable written buy-sell agreement, these doctors have defaulted to a strategy that amounts to "someone will sell my practice after I'm dead." The sale, when it does happen, usually falls as a surprise to the spouse and children, who have to step in and sell the practice after the owner passes away.

It's important that the doctor's personal financial plan has a strategy to efficiently turn a sale of the practice into retirement income. At this stage of the game, the doctor needs to understand where the income will come from in each and every year throughout retirement—which accounts, which funds. What will be sold, and when and how much will be there? Is there a safety factor?

Many doctors overestimate the value of their practice. This tends to throw the whole retirement plan into disarray. If the doctor has been expecting to get a million dollars for the dental office and finds out that it is worth perhaps only half a million dollars, then the assumptions of the retirement plan and expected lifestyle will greatly change.

In summary, the doctor needs a financial plan driven by goals. The financial planning process should direct the business plan to produce a result. The business should fund the doctor's lifestyle and provide enough additional cash flow to reinvest in the practice to grow it and improve patient care, with enough money left over to fund investments outside of the practice to meet the doctor's long-term financial goals.

Personal goals drive the financial plan, and the financial plan makes demands on the practice. Business planning drives the achievement of collections. As a dental practice owner, the doctor is solely responsible for making sure that the financial plan and the business plan are congruent.

Thriving doctors must focus to keep their work and home lives in balance. Just as it's important for the upper teeth to fit well with the lower teeth, so it's important for the doctor's business and personal lives to mesh.

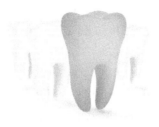

CHAPTER 13

GETTING READY FOR GOOD-BYE

There are four basic ways of getting out of the business of owning a practice to create a liquidity event—if that is what the doctor intends to do. The doctor might decide to keep it in the family and gift it to a son or daughter who is a dentist. That happens, although not too often.

1. Generally, the dental practice is not kept forever. It might just shut down as the doctor gets older, slows down, and lets production slip, eventually just selling the equipment and perhaps the patient charts to another practice. Or the doctor might die while operating the practice. The surviving spouse will need to step in and sell the practice before the staff and patients leave and its value plummets to a fraction of what was expected.

2. The doctor could sell the practice to a third party, to another doctor, or to a corporation. This could be done when the doctor is alive and ready to retire or after his death. Certainly, selling the practice is what most doctors envision; it's just that they don't plan it nearly as well as they could.

3. Another option is hiring a junior dentist, an associate, who will take over the dental office and buy the doctor out over time. For many, this option seems the best: The doctor, while moving from five to three days a week, hires somebody who does all the work that he or she doesn't want to do. Meanwhile, the associate is paying some money over time as the doctor wades into retirement.

   The problem is that most doctors are just not wired to do that sort of grooming of a successor. They have run their own dental office for years and years, they are used to getting their way, and they are not used to sharing authority, risk, and responsibility. So when a new doctor comes in, conflict arises. The senior doctor may want to keep all the money, do things only his way, take only the cases he wants, and deal with people in a way that makes the junior doctor feel uncomfortable. For the seller, this play-it-by-ear option might seem ideal, but it could be the most difficult to pull off.

4. Another option is to expand to multiple associates in multiple offices. The advantages of a multi-doctor practice are significant. From a cash flow basis, these doctors tend to make more, because they have lower average costs: they use the same office to treat more

patients. They also have more flexibility to meet staff and patient needs. They might be able to do some specialty work, as each doctor focuses on what he or she does best. That creates economies of scale.

Also, the advantage of having multiple doctors in a single practice is that each is able to sell part of the practice to a new arrival. That way, while still working, a doctor can sell a business asset that is growing at practice's historical rate of collections growth, and use that money to fund a more diversified and tax-favored investment outside of the practice, such as a retirement plan or a defined benefit pension plan, that is potentially growing at a higher rate of return.

Although a multiple-doctor practice has the potential of lower overhead, it needs very strong business systems in place to actually realize that lower overhead and to control costs. The doctors must be able to delegate key responsibilities, such as hiring, training, clinical procedures to be done, and advertising.

STRATEGIES THAT YOU CAN LIVE WITH

A common situation is the doctor who owns a dental practice and building and has one or two hygienists, some front desk staff, and dental assistants. The doctor might be a specialist but isn't in a group practice.

Whatever strategy the doctor has for transitioning the dental practice, it should work seamlessly with the personal financial plan. The doctor's individual goals have deadlines, and those goals drive the personal financial plan, and that needs to drive the business model. Certainly, the business model must take into account the sale of the business and the transition into the doctor's retirement.

The doctor must know, before negotiating, the minimum price needed as a result of the practice sale for the financial plan to work. If the discussions drift below that number, the doctor can halt the negotiations and either reevaluate or find a new buyer.

The doctor must also understand, from a personal financial aspect, the terms of the deal. It's not just about the valuation of the practice and the price or whether there will be an agreement for the doctor to stay on during the transition. What will the income look like? Will there be a rental agreement for the building? What are the tax implications? Doctors must understand the key aspects of their personal financial situation. They need to know what helps them and hurts them.

They also need to know what to do with the money. Will the sale proceeds be used to pay off debts? Will it be invested? Or will it just go into the bank for living expenses? Doctors must figure this out. They have spent a lot of time building a practice and should have a good idea why they are retiring. They need to do it on their own terms and make the most of it.

There should be a detailed map for the personal cash flow for at least the next ten years. How much money will be needed for various purposes—for insurance, lifestyle, vacations, and education of the grandchildren? How will debts and taxes be paid? A financial plan will map out how much money will be needed every year. It will establish when the doctor will begin to get Social Security benefits and when the spouse will apply.

Doctors who will be spending down assets to fund their retirement lifestyle should know the right combination for pulling assets from an IRA, a brokerage, or a Roth account. What will be the source of money from year to year? What makes the most sense? The sequencing of withdrawals matters in a retirement strategy.

Which debts will be paid first? What about the debt on the building? If the building isn't going to be sold, will the doctor pay off the mortgage or keep the debt? Will the doctor have a home mortgage?

All of these considerations need to be factored in as to what makes sense based on the doctor's goals and situation. These variables all need to be addressed, as well as taking a hard look at the doctor's personal budget.

THE TOUGH QUESTIONS

Before selling the business, doctors should be asking themselves some tough questions and looking for flaws in their planning assumptions.

- What if I have an extended health-care event that could burn through a lot of cash right as I retire?

- If all of my money is invested in the stock market when I retire, what will happen if there is a bear market and I have to sell something at a loss to pay household expenses?

- Is there room for error, or do my investments have to work out perfectly every year in order to maintain my lifestyle?

- If I agree to finance the buyer's purchase of my practice, what happens to my lifestyle if the buyer can't keep up with the payments?

- Do I still need life insurance? What will I do for health insurance until I am eligible for Medicare at age 65? Will I need a Medicare supplement? Long-term-care insurance? Liability insurance?

- What will I do with the rest of my time? What am I planning to do in retirement?

Doctors must address all of those issues before they sell. They certainly don't want to be winging it as they go into retirement.

A MULTIYEAR APPROACH

When the time comes to sell the practice, doctors must take a multiyear approach. Instead of slowing down, they need to focus on maximizing cash flow. They need to focus on earning as much money as possible until retirement day. Doing so will make the dental practice worth the most it could ever be worth.

The buyer will want to see that written procedures and systems are set up and that the staff is trained. Those are strong signals to a buyer that the practice is a good investment. Doctors who are renting their dental office should renegotiate the lease or at least read the lease agreement to verify that it can pass on to the new buyer without a significant change in the office lease's favorable terms. In addition, what sprucing up of the office must be done? Is the staff prepared? How will the doctor fund retirement plans in the last couple of years before retiring? All this must be considered from a multiyear perspective.

The seller may be planning to upgrade equipment to satisfy the needs of the buyer or what the doctor thinks the buyer might want. If so, this must be done strategically, not willy-nilly. Certainly, everything in the office must be fully functional so that the buyer doesn't have any issues about a broken chair, broken hand pieces, or an air conditioner that is about to conk out.

The seller must have formal financial statements and a statement of production for the buyer for at least three to five years. That includes the profit and loss statements, the statement of net worth, and the cash flow statement. A CPA generally produces these. As discussed in the previous chapter, the doctor must have a formal valuation of the practice. The buyer will need that to get a loan, and the buyer will need the production history to be confident of enjoying similar benefits of ownership.

The doctor must find a buyer and will probably need more than one candidate. The doctor may find an associate to take over but will need a replacement buyer in case that person backs out. Doctors who do not have a committed buyer lined up will probably need to engage a business broker to sell the practice. How will the business broker be vetted? Will he just call some number on the back of a dental journal or on a website? Does he even know what to ask? What will the broker do? What does it cost? How long will it take? Are there any guarantees?

It will also be important to have a CPA involved and an attorney to draft the documents for the sale and the prospectus for the practice. The doctor must set the price and be able to propose favorable terms. For example, will the seller work in the practice or walk away? Will there be an agreement not to compete?

Then the doctor must be able to confidently negotiate the sale. This is the dental practice that provided the income to support the doctor's family. It paid off the house. It put the children through school—and now, it will provide for retirement.

GOOD TIME TO DELEGATE

As with anything else, the doctor can do these tasks himself, delegate them, or leave them undone. But to meet a retirement date, all of this work must be done and done correctly. Nothing important should be ignored. Doctors who are not going to do these things themselves must hire somebody to help.

The doctor needs trusted advisors throughout the process. A CERTIFIED FINANCIAL PLANNER™ Professional can help to figure out what the sale of the business would mean for the doctor and the approach that would make the most sense. A CPA can help with the financial statements and advise from a tax point of view. An attorney can draft and negotiate terms, a non-compete agreement or a consulting agreement. The doctor also might need a business broker to identify buyers and close the sale. You may need a dental equipment sales rep for strategic technology improvements and a building contractor for repairs to the office. And a dental practice management consultant can help to maximize cash flow.

Dentists generally don't clean teeth. They are trained to do so, but they don't. They have hygienists. Time is money. The doctor is the only one who can do the corrective dentistry and the only one who can lead the business, so spending time cleaning teeth takes time away from that more productive work.

If doctors take the approach that it is best to delegate some tasks, even those that they are trained to do, then it makes sense to delegate tasks that they are not trained to do—such as accounting, legal work, selling a business, negotiating real estate deals, or figuring out nuanced retirement options. It's best for doctors to be in a role where everybody comes to them with a coordinated plan of attack that they can then validate as consistent with what they want to do.

CONCLUSION

MONEY WHERE YOUR MOUTH IS

Most of the ideas, strategies, and tools that I've developed could be described as "universal in their application" or ones that "will work for any dentist." Two things, at least, are wrong with this conclusion. One, your situation, dental practice, goals, fears, family, and those that you care about are unique. Consequently, they require a focused, congruent, and tailored plan. Second, a universal approach by definition disregards the personality of the dentist seeking advice as though these strategies were a "plug and play" affair.

As a dentist, you have needs, wants, and goals—like all human beings. You should focus on identifying what is important to you personally and professionally. You need smart, targeted financial goals that have dates and numbers associated with them.

Your financial plan should relate what you need to do on a year-by-year basis to achieve those financial goals. From buying insurance to paying down debt to investing in a retirement plan, you need to know which levers to pull, when to pull them, and how hard. That is what your financial plan should do.

Most financial planners focus on the demand side of the personal financial plan. If you are not saving enough to retire at 55, the planner instead will propose retiring at 65—or downsizing your retirement expectations. You either have to cut back, wait, or invest more aggressively. That's the traditional financial planning approach.

My approach is to look at your professional practice and business model to find the money. How else can you maintain your lifestyle while saving sufficient money to achieve your financial goals? How are you adjusting your business to make that happen? Instead, develop a "lifestyle" dental practice. Through financial planning, you, your business consultant, and your staff will be able to see what you must produce each year to achieve all your personal and professional objectives.

You must figure out how much money you need to save and how to get it. Early in a dental career, it is highly important to save as much as possible. Toward the middle part of a career, the planning must focus on making sure that you are not taking too much risk and will be able to transition out of dentistry into retirement without stress.

That requires a multiyear strategy for paying off debt. It will take at least six or seven years and probably more like 15. But if you wait 15 years to start saving any money, you might have no debt, but you will also be illiquid. If you have all your money tied up in your practice you may never be able to retire.

You must take immediate steps if you have not implemented these strategies. Even if you can't solve everything today, you must start now, because if you wait too long, it's almost impossible to compensate, and you will fail. You will not be able to achieve the standard of living that you desire while working or in retirement.

You should have a CERTIFIED FINANCIAL PLANNER™ Professional on your team. The CFP designation is the gold standard of financial planning in the United States. Most dentists believe that their financial advisor is certified; unfortunately, many times this is not the case. If the planner is not a CFP, he or she lacks the basic levels of knowledge, experience, or ethical standards, and he or she should not be working with you. If you do have a qualified planner with whom you want to discuss these issues, please pass this book on to that person. Ask that person some specific questions about what you have learned in these pages, and find out how he or she might deal with those issues. Their response to your questions will better help you to decide if you need to bring some other people on board.

My dedication to dentists is personal, based on my experiences growing up in a dentist's home. I find great satisfaction in seeing dentists reach financial success. It breaks my heart when I come across a doctor who has worked hard for decades, yet cannot maintain a standard of dignity after leaving the profession. Much of my life's work has been committed to helping dentists like you to be as successful as possible in the least stressful way, consistent with the honest and ethical values that you share.

Printed in the USA
CPSIA information can be obtained
at www.ICGtesting.com
JSHW012036140824
68134JS00033B/3097

9 781599 325309